Chūshingura

(The Treasury of Loyal Retainers)

Prepared for the Columbia College Program of Translations from
the Asian Classics   WM. THEODORE DE BARY, Editor

Chūshingura

(The Treasury of Loyal Retainers)

A Puppet Play

by

TAKEDA IZUMO, MIYOSHI SHŌRAKU
and NAMIKI SENRYŪ

Translated by Donald Keene

Columbia University Press / New York

se at Columbia University,
ys of *Chikamatsu* (1961)
surezuregusa *of Kenkō*)
Plays of the Nō Theatre
(1970).

Portions of this work were prepared under a grant from the Carnegie Corporation of New York and under a contract with the U. S. Office of Education for the production of texts to be used in undergraduate education. The draft translations so produced have been used in the Columbia College Oriental Humanities program and have subsequently been revised and expanded for publication in the present form. Copyright is claimed only in those portions of the work not included in the draft translations delivered under the contract with the U. S. Office of Education. Neither the Carnegie Corporation nor the U. S. Office of Education is the author, owner, publisher, or proprietor of this publication, and neither is to be understood as approving by virtue of its support any of the statements made or views expressed therein.

UNESCO Collection of Representative Works
Japanese Series
This book
has been accepted
in the Japanese Series
of the Translations Collection
of the United Nations
Educational, Scientific and Cultural Organization
(UNESCO)

This translation is dedicated to
Yukio Mishima

"Kuni osamatte yoki bushi no chū mo buyū mo kakururu ni,
tatoeba hoshi no hiru miezu yoru wa midarete arawaruru."

Contents

Foreword

THE *Chūshingura* is one of the Translations from the Oriental Classics prepared under the sponsorship of the Committee on Oriental Studies in order to bring to Western readers representative works of the major Asian traditions in thought and literature. Our intention is to provide translations based on scholarly study but written for the general reader, and especially for undergraduates in general education courses, rather than primarily for other specialists.

The standing of the *Chūshingura* as probably the classic work of the Japanese puppet and kabuki theater derives from its continuing popularity with the Japanese people over the years. This popularity has survived the vicissitudes of war and politics, and the misinterpretations or misrepresentations of those who saw in it nothing but a warlike and militaristic spirit. No doubt the prevalence of this view, especially during the war years and the occupation, discouraged anyone from attempting a more adequate translation or reprinting earlier ones. Fortunately Professor Keene has been willing to apply his prodigious talents as a translator of Japanese literature to the task of making this a classic for Western readers as well as for Japanese.

Wm. Theodore de Bary

Preface to the
Second Paperback Edition

IN 1905, at the time of the negotiations conducted in Portsmouth, New Hampshire to conclude the Russo-Japanese War, President Theodore Roosevelt, who was serving as the mediator, struck some observers as being pro-Japanese despite his professed neutrality. This partiality (if real) may perhaps be explained in terms of his admiration for the ideals of the Japanese as depicted in the play *Chūshingura*, which he had read in translation years earlier. The story of the vendetta carried out by forty-seven *rōnin* (masterless samurai) who remained faithful to the memory of their former master captured the imagination of many people in the West, even those who knew nothing else about Japan. In the editions of the *Encyclopaedia Britannica* published during the decades prior to the 1950s the only article devoted to a Japanese literary work was on "The Forty-Seven Rōnin."

Chūshingura (The Treasury of Loyal Retainers) was originally composed in 1748 as a play for the puppet theater. At this time the major Japanese dramatists were writing their plays for puppets rather than actors, a choice often attributed to dissatisfaction with the liberties that Kabuki actors often took with the texts. The operators of the puppets, having no personalities or special dramatic skills of their own to display before the public (at the expense of the texts), could be trusted to perform the plays as written. The success of the puppet version of *Chūshingura* when first staged was so overwhelming that it did not take long for the Kabuki playwrights to adapt the play for their own purposes, making changes in the text in order to exploit the expressive potential of the actors and the attraction of their individual faces. Two centuries later the play was modified even more drastically to meet the demands of film and television, and this process will no doubt continue in years to come.

There surely cannot be many Japanese who have never heard of *Chūshingura* or the events that inspired the play, though only a comparative few have actually read the original text. Books continue to be published about *Chūshingura*, not only scholarly studies of the style, the authorship, and similar aspects of the text but also popular works, some debunking the presentation of the events, others explaining the hold *Chūshingura* continues to exert over the Japanese public. I have even heard an explanation of the popularity of Beethoven's Ninth Symphony in Japan in terms of the structural similarities it shares with *Chūshingura!*

During the immediate postwar years (from 1945), the American Army of Occupation forbade performances of *Chūshingura* because it glorified militarism and was feudalistic in its insistence on such outmoded concepts as honor and loyalty. The ban was eventually lifted, but in 1960, at the time of the first Kabuki performances in the United States, members of the Japanese Diet opposed the inclusion of *Chūshingura* in the repertory, fearing that American audiences might suppose the action was representative of contemporary Japan. Such fears were eventually overcome, and *Chūshingura* (or at least sections of this extremely long play) was successfully performed abroad, transcending the centuries and the immense physical distance. It is a work of which the Japanese—and the rest of the world—can feel proud.

Donald Keene

Preface

THE MOST famous and popular work in the entire Japanese theatrical repertory is, beyond any doubt, *Chūshingura*, "The Treasury of Loyal Retainers." The play itself (and the numerous adaptations made since it was first created in 1748) together with the historical and legendary materials surrounding the story of the vendetta have become part of the heritage of the Japanese people. Surely there cannot be many Japanese unfamiliar with the story and its heroes, even if they are quite unaware that *Chūshingura* was first written as a puppet play. It has again and again been made into films and, more recently, into television dramas; in whatever medium it continues to exert an undiminished attraction for the Japanese public.

The full title of the play is *Kanadehon Chūshingura*. The first word means "a copybook of *kana*," a penmanship book for writing the forty-seven symbols making up the Japanese syllabary. The title calls attention to the coincidence between the number of *kana* and the number of heroes who took part in the vendetta (if we include one man who was only an honorary participant). There are references to this coincidence, especially in the last act. *Kanadehon* also suggests that the play was written in *kana*, simple Japanese, rather than the high-flown style of the Confucian philosophers who praised the immortal forty-seven. But only pedants now use the full title of the play; for the innumerable spectators the title is simply *Chūshingura*, and so it shall be called here.

I have presented a complete translation of the original text. However, it should not be forgotten that it was written as a *jōruri*, or puppet play, and the musical accompaniment was an integral part of the performance. The lines, whether declaimed or sung by one or more chanters, were never delivered in the flat tones of ordinary conversation. The musical element unquestionably deserves special treatment, but I am not sufficiently versed in these matters to say more than that the music heightens the effect of almost every scene. I hope that some trained musician will illuminate for us this aspect of *Chūshingura*.

In making this translation, together with the study of the background material given in the Introduction, I was in receipt of a grant from the U. S. Office of Education, for which I hereby express my deep thanks. The grant enabled me not only to study the texts but to see performances of *Chūshingura*, both by Kabuki actors and by puppets, that added much to my understanding of the play.

I am grateful also to Mr. Torigoe Bunzō of Waseda University for the generous help he gave with problems in the text. Annotated editions of *Chūshingura* are miserably inadequate, and I have been lucky to have had a friend to whom I could turn for assistance.

Chūshingura is a grand apotheosis of samurai ideals. These ideals have in recent times been held up to doubt, and reading the work today we may sometimes feel slightly uncomfortable. Nevertheless, it stands as a monument of Japanese popular drama, a work of eternal appeal.

Donald Keene
Tokyo–New York

Chūshingura

(The Treasury of Loyal Retainers)

Introduction

ON THE NIGHT of the fourteenth day of the twelfth month of the fifteenth year of Genroku, or January 30, 1703, by the Western calendar, forty-six former retainers of the late Lord Asano Naganori of Akō burst into the mansion of Lord Kira Yoshinaka in Edo and killed him. They immediately carried his head to Sengaku-ji, the Buddhist temple where Asano was buried, and offered it before his grave. With this act their vendetta was completed.

News of these events spread rapidly. Almost at once people started to refer to the forty-six *rōnin* ("wave men," or masterless samurai) as *gishi* (righteous warriors), a term plainly indicating approval of their deed. It was generally agreed that the murder of Kira Yoshinaka had been justified by the events of twenty-one months earlier. Asano, an inexperienced country baron entrusted with the reception of an imperial envoy from Kyoto, had been instructed to seek guidance from Kira, an expert in court ceremonials. He failed to provide Kira with the expected bribe, and Kira taunted the younger man until at last Asano lost his temper, drew his sword, and slashed him. The wounds were superficial, but Tsunayoshi, the shogun, was so outraged by this

1

unseemly breach of decorum in the palace that he commanded Asano to commit suicide. His lands were also confiscated, and his retainers set adrift as *rōnin*. Kira naturally
feared reprisals, and his spies kept watch on Asano's men,
but the forty-six conspirators, led by Ōishi Kuranosuke, the
senior retainer, bided their time. When at last they struck
they penetrated Kira's defenses.

The boldness of the vendetta caught the imagination of
people of every class. At a time when the samurai ideals of
loyalty and resolute action seemed to have been forgotten,
thanks to the peace of almost a hundred years, this sudden
dramatic gesture came as a heartening reminder of what
being a samurai had once meant. Even the Confucian scholars, normally pacific men, were moved to admiration, remembering the old teaching that a man should not permit
his father's enemy to live under the same sky as himself.
They further declared that the forty-six loyal retainers perfectly embodied the highest ideals of the virtuous man. Numerous poems and essays, mainly in Chinese, were composed
to commemorate and glorify the forty-six heroes.

But not all the Confucianists approved of the vendetta.
Ogyū Sorai, the greatest philosopher of the time, expressed
his reservations soon after the events:

By righteousness we mean the path of keeping oneself free from
any taint, and by law we mean the measuring rod for the entire
country. A man controls his heart with decorum and his actions
with righteousness. For the forty-six samurai to have avenged
their master on this occasion shows that they are aware of
shame, as becomes men who are samurai; and since they have
followed the path of keeping themselves free from taint, their
deed is righteous. However, this deed is appropriate only to
their particular group; it amounts therefore to a special excep-
tion to the rules. The persons connected with the vendetta con-

sidered Kira to be their enemy because Asano Naganori was punished for his disorderly behavior in the palace, and they deliberately planned an act of violence without official permission. This is not to be tolerated under the law. If the forty-six samurai are pronounced guilty and condemned to commit *seppuku*, in keeping with the traditions of the samurai, the claim of the Uesugi family [1] will be satisfied, and the loyalty of the men will not have been disparaged. This must therefore be considered as a general principle. If general principles are impaired by special exceptions, there will no longer be any respect for the law in this country.[2]

Other Confucianists were of the opinion that the action of the forty-six samurai could not be considered a vendetta in the true sense of the word because the injured party in the original dispute was Kira, not Asano.[3] The shogun, impressed especially by Sorai's reasoning, finally decided that the men must die, and on March 20, 1703, they committed *seppuku*, the ritual disembowelment. Their bodies also were interred in the Sengaku-ji, and their graves have ever since been a place of pilgrimage.

Two weeks after the loyal *rōnin* were buried *Akebono Soga no Youchi* (Night attack at dawn by the Soga) was staged at the Nakamura Theater in Edo. The authorities closed the play after three performances. Nothing survives of the contents, but the title suggests that, under the pretext of describing the celebrated night attack of the twelfth-century Soga brothers, broad references had been made to the assault on Kira's mansion by the forty-six *rōnin*. Censorship of the theater at the time prohibited the dramatization of matters of contemporary political interest, but this rule

[1] Kira Yoshinaka's wife was from the highly influential Uesugi family.

[2] *Akō Gijin Sansho*, supplementary volume, p. 150.

[3] Matsushima Eiichi, *Chūshingura*, pp. 128–30.

was often circumvented by changing the setting of the
events to the distant past and by disguising the names of the
participants. Apparently the 1703 Kabuki play was too close
to the events for even such dodges to succeed, and the discouraged Kabuki actors did not quickly attempt another
work on the vendetta theme.

The oldest surviving play on the vendetta was *Goban
Taiheiki* (A chronicle of great peace played on a chessboard), written in 1706 by the great dramatist Chikamatsu
Monzaemon. Less than a month earlier he had written a
puppet play called *Kenkō Hōshi Monomiguruma* (The sight-
seeing carriage of the priest Kenkō) which describes how
Kenkō, famed as the author of *Tsurezuregusa* (*Essays in
Idleness*), attempted to help a court lady who was the
object of the unwanted attentions of the general Kō no
Moronao. Kenkō persuaded Moronao to shift his attentions
to Kaoyo, the wife to Enya Hangan, but she rejected his
suit. Moronao, greatly annoyed, denounced Kaoyo's husband
and forced him to commit *seppuku*. The play, in two acts
instead of the customary three, ended at this point, and
probably seemed incomplete. A few weeks later Chikamatsu
supplied a third act with a title of its own, *Goban Taiheiki*.
The three acts hang together as well as those of many other
puppet plays, but oddly enough they were not performed
on the same bill. Perhaps this was because Chikamatsu had
changed his conception of the work once he decided to write
an act that treated, more or less openly, the vendetta of
Asano's loyal retainers.

Goban Taiheiki, on the surface at least, is a continuation
of a play about Kō no Moronao, a historical figure of the
fourteenth century; its "world" (*sekai*) is therefore set in the
same period. This accidental circumstance determined the

period for most subsequent versions of the story. In brief, Chikamatsu's play tells the following story: A *rōnin* of Enya Hangan has changed his name to Ōboshi Yuranosuke and is living in retirement with his son Rikiya in Yamashina. He receives frequent messages from his confederates, other *rōnin* who had served under Enya, saying that the time is ripe to attack Moronao's mansion in Kamakura. Rikiya's suspicions are aroused by the behavior of a servant named Okahei. Supposing the man is a spy sent by Moronao, he wounds him, but Okahei reveals with his dying breath that he is in fact Teraoka Heiemon, a loyal retainer of Enya's. In order to calm Moronao's fears of vengeance, he has pretended to be a spy, and has reported that Yuranosuke and Rikiya are so given to debauchery that they will surely not attempt a vendetta. Yuranosuke promises to include Heiemon posthumously in the league, and the dying man plots on a chessboard, with black and white *go* stones, the layout of Moronao's mansion. Yuranosuke is enabled by this information to complete his preparations. In the second scene he and his men successfully attack and, cutting off Moronao's head, offer it before their master's grave. They all commit *seppuku* together.[4]

The close connections between this play and *Chūshingura* are evident. Not only are both works set in the same period, but the names of many characters are also the same. The villainous Kira is identified by Chikamatsu with Kō no Moronao (d. 1351), and Lord Asano with Enya Hangan, killed in 1350 as the result of Moronao's plotting. The name of Asano's retainer, Ōishi Kuranosuke, slightly altered by Chikamatsu to Ōboshi Yuranosuke, so remained in *Chūshingura*. Various other names retained forms Chikamatsu

---

[4] Text in Takano Masami, ed., *Chikamatsu Monzaemon Shū*, II, 29–57. An English translation of the play *Goban Taiheiki* made by Jacqueline Muller was published in the *Harvard Journal of Asiatic Studies*.

had used, as did the main incidents—Enya's suicide as the result of Moronao's machinations, the inclusion of a dead man among the participants in the vendetta, and the final success of the assault on Moronao's mansion. *Goban Taiheiki*, a one-act play, naturally lacked the complexities that won for *Chūshingura* its lasting popularity, and is today never performed; nevertheless, it provided the core of the later work.

It may be wondered how Chikamatsu managed to evade the censorship that had shut down the Kabuki play of 1703. The lapse of three years undoubtedly made the authorities less nervous about the possible repercussions of a play on the subject. Moreover, the censorship was apparently less strict in the Kyoto-Osaka region than in Edo.[5] Chikamatsu's careful identification of the characters with historical figures of the distant past probably also allayed the censor's fears; in Tokugawa Japan, even when it came to censorship, the form, rather than the actuality, was the object of greatest concern.

During the years between 1706, when Chikamatsu's *Goban Taiheiki* appeared, and 1748, when *Chūshingura* was written, many playwrights, for both the Kabuki and puppet theaters, tried their hand at writing works on the theme of the loyal forty-six (or forty-seven, if the honorary member of the league was included). The plays grew longer, in keeping with current fashions in the theater, leading to a proliferation of subplots and minor characters. The general outlines of the vendetta remained the same, regardless of the dramatist, but the period was sometimes shifted to the late-fifteenth century, necessitating a change in the names of the characters, and such details as the exact cause of the original quarrel between Asano and Kira varied considerably. Hardly

[5] Matsushima, p. 134.

a year went by without a new play on the theme. Even the works that were quickly forgotten sometimes provided elements of the plots of later plays, including *Chūshingura*. The character Hayano Kampei, for example, first appeared in *Chūshin Kogane no Tanzaku* (Loyal retainers, a golden poem card) a puppet play written in 1732 by Namiki Sōsuke (1695–1751). The same man, under the name Namiki Senryū, was to be one of the three authors of *Chūshingura*. Sixteen years later he returned to this earlier play for some of his materials.

Whatever the merits of the many plays about the loyal retainers composed before and after *Chūshingura*, there can be no question that it was the finest. Even adaptations for the films or television that cater to modern tastes by adding details of motivation and character that would have been incomprehensible to an eighteenth-century audience follow in general the story of *Chūshingura* and sometimes even retain sections of the original dialogue. It may seem curious that dramatists continued to turn out variations on the theme of the vendetta even after the appearance of this masterpiece, but the public's appetite for plays about the immortal *rōnin* was insatiable, and novelty (as well as excellence) was always demanded. Yet even as the new plays multiplied, the reputation of *Chūshingura* as a classic steadily grew.

Authorship

The composition of *Chūshingura* doubtless began with a conference of the three dramatists to decide on the outlines of the plot and assign responsibility for the different acts. The names of these men are given at the end of the play: Takeda Izumo, Miyoshi Shōraku, Namiki Senryū. Normally, in the case of multiple authorship the name of the principal playwright was given first, and the next highest ranked playwright last. If this was true of *Chūshingura*, we may infer that Takeda Izumo planned and supervised the entire play and wrote most of the important acts, the sixth, ninth, fourth, and first. Miyoshi Shōraku probably wrote the least important, the second, tenth, and eleventh acts.[6]

Our best source of clues to the authorship is the short critical work *Chūshingura Okame Hyōban* by the celebrated fiction writer Jippensha Ikku (1765–1831).[7] Although written in 1803, more than fifty years after the first performance of *Chūshingura*, its various anecdotes have a ring of authenticity. Ikku states (or strongly implies) that Miyoshi Shōraku wrote the second and tenth acts, Namiki Senryū the fourth, and Takeda Izumo the ninth; this would in general conform to what we might expect. If a few guesses may be allowed, it seems likely that Izumo wrote the sixth and seventh acts, and Senryū the third.

Takeda Izumo II (1691–1756) was ranked by Jippensha Ikku on equal terms with Chikamatsu as a dramatist; even if few people share this view today, it is undeniable that he and various collaborators wrote the most popular plays in the entire literature of the puppet stage, including *Natsumatsuri Naniwa Kagami* (1745), *Sugawara Denju Tenarai Kagami* [8]

---

[6] The analysis of the relative importance of acts of a five-act *jōruri* play was made by Yokoyama Tadashi in *Jōruri Ayatsuri Shibai no Kenkyū*, p. 593. The equation of the five acts of a normal play with the eleven acts of *Chūshingura* may be found in Toita Yasuji: *Chūshingura*, p. 106.

[7] Jippensha Ikku is known especially as the author of *Hizakurige*, of which there is an English translation by Thomas Satchell.

[8] A free translation of this play is included in Earle Ernst, *Three Japanese Plays*.

(1746), and *Yoshitsune Sembonzakura* (1747). Namiki Senryū (1695–1751) was an equally skilled playwright, as we know from works written independently, like *Ichinotani Futaba Gunki* (1751).[9] But Miyoshi Shōraku (1696–1772) was apparently no more than a competent hack; certainly the second and tenth acts of the play are inferior to the others. Ikku relates a revealing anecdote about Shōraku:

When the author, Miyoshi Shōraku, had written this section [of the second act], a disciple working with him asked, "There is a phrase in the text saying that Honzō swore an oath by ringing the metal of one sword on another, so clearly he must have had his own swords. Why, then, should he have taken up his master's dirk and drawn it from its scabbard? Moreover, it was surely a gross breach of etiquette to polish the dirk which, after all, stands for the master's soul, with a straw sandal. How do you justify this?" Shōraku was extremely stubborn by nature, and even if something did not seem reasonable, even to himself, he would never correct it if anyone else criticized it. It was his way never to compromise in the slightest on anything once he had put it down on paper; so, not deigning to make an answer, he left the phrase exactly as it was. The disciple persisted and asked once more. This time Shōraku flew into a rage and said, "It's nothing you could appreciate. You shouldn't bring up matters that are none of your business." The disciple therefore said no more.

When the play was eventually staged, a man named Yoshida Senzō operated the puppet for Honzō. He performed the part exactly as Shōraku had written it: Honzō took his master's dirk, folded a straw sandal to polish it, then cut off a branch from the pine tree. The same disciple, seeing the performance, thought that surely there must be some reason for this action, and took the opportunity to ask Shōraku, who answered, "If any of you younger people had written a passage like that, the

[9] The most famous scene of this work, *Kumagai Jinya* (Kumagai's camp) is still frequently performed.

chanter would certainly have criticized it and refused to recite it. The same would undoubtedly have been true of the puppet operator too. It's because *I* wrote it that even a famous operator performed it exactly as written without any protest. If you work very hard someday you'll be able to write such illogical things too." [10]

The unevenness of the play no doubt resulted from the collaboration of three men of unequal abilities, but it would be premature to assign the superior acts to Izumo or Senryū and the inferior ones to Shōraku; as yet no attempt has been made to determine the authorship on the basis of stylistic features or characteristic plot techniques.

The multiple authorship is presumably to blame also for the noticeable inconsistencies in the characters. Sagisaka Bannai, for example, is a comical character in the third act, but by the seventh act there is hardly a trace left of his comicality, and at the end of the play the triumph of the loyal retainers is climaxed by killing Bannai, as if he, rather than Moronao, were the chief villain. Again, Kakogawa Honzō fawningly offering bribes to Moronao in the third act by no means appears the same man as the heroic Honzō of the ninth act; as a result, two different actors commonly take the role when the complete play is performed. The same holds true of Rikiya; the blushing young man of the second act is so unlike the resolute hero of the ninth act as to require two actors. It often happens in Kabuki that the same actor will assume several roles in a play, as a display of his virtuosity, and this is true also of *Chūshingura*.[11] But for two actors to assume the same role suggests that not even a

---

[10] Jippensha Ikku, *Chūshingura Okame Hyōban*, pp. 438–39.

[11] For example, the roles of Enya Hangan and Okaru are often both taken by Onoe Baikō.

virtuoso actor could encompass the widely differing concep-
tions of the character.

Chūshingura is nevertheless one of the rare puppet plays
still staged more or less in entirety, though it takes ten or
eleven hours to perform. Despite the inconsistencies and the
scenes of inferior inspiration, the story of the vendetta unfolds with a magnificent cumulative effect. The play is
marked also by the great variety of its scenes. Even similar
situations, such as the suicides of Enya Hangan and of
Kampei, should produce quite different impressions.[12] For all
the shortcomings that may be attributed to the multiple
authorship, this variety of effects, important especially in a
theater of wooden-faced puppets, may have been the fortunate product of collaboration.

Characters and Style

The fact that *Chūshingura* was originally a puppet play
may account for a tendency towards stereotypes in the characters. With only a limited variety of puppet heads available
—bad, middle-aged man, good young woman, righteous old
man, etc.—shadings in characterization were difficult to
achieve. Is it possible, for example, to differentiate the three
virtuous wives, Tonase, Oishi, and Osono? Though their
situations are different, each of them is a paragon of feminine
virtue, ready to give up her life without a second thought if

12 Ikku relates how one puppet operator criticized another for not
maintaining the distinction in attitude between Enya Hangan and
Wakasanosuke when each man is insulted by Moronao. The operator
in question made the puppet for Enya clutch his sword and tremble
all over with suppressed wrath, but this was not justified by the text,
which reserves such descriptions for Wakasanosuke. Enya Hangan
should listen quietly, looking down, until one final straw breaks the
back of his samurai calm. Thus, even two very similar scenes must
be carefully distinguished in performance. (See Jippensha, p. 440.)

her death will serve her husband. In puppet performances
the three roles would be played with identical puppet heads
and distinguished only by costuming, as much as to suggest
that external circumstances, rather than their characters,
distinguished them. Some characters, it is true, are more
complicated, but this is usually less the result of internal
contradictions than of clumsy editing of the work of three
authors. Most of the characters are either wholly good,
without even a tragic flaw, or wholly bad, without a redeeming grace. This tends to make them seem two-dimen-
sional, but greater subtlety was beyond the expressive capa-
bilities of the puppets. In any case, much that may seem un-
satisfactory in reading performs extremely well.

Jippensha Ikku, praising what he called the "Takeda style"
displayed in Chūshingura, contrasted it with Chikamatsu's
dramas. In a typical play by Chikamatsu, he says, it is only
towards the end that the spectator first learns the truth about
a character. If, then, Chikamatsu had written Chūshingura,
Yuranosuke would have remained dissolute throughout the
seventh act scene in the Ichiriki Teahouse, and revealed his
true colors only in the ninth act, at his retreat in Yamashina.
Takeda Izumo, on the other hand, did not hesitate to show
Yuranosuke for the first time in the seventh act as a dissolute
reveler, and then disclose that his antics were a sham intended to deceive Moronao's spies, only to have Yuranosuke
pretend to be dissolute once again in the ninth act. This
shifting back and forth in the characterization seemed to
Jippensha Ikku typical of Takeda Izumo's style; the changes
and variety kept the audience ever from becoming bored.
The failure of Chikamatsu's plays to hold the stage (except
in the drastically revised versions of later men), despite their
literary excellence, seems to confirm Ikku's judgments. The
audiences clearly enjoyed the unrelieved somberness of a

Chikamatsu tragedy much less than the lively variety in Izumo's plays, which compensated for any inadequacies in the characterization.

Ikku also contrasted the long speeches delivered by Chikamatsu's characters with the rapid exchanges of dialogue typical of *Chūshingura*. Even the parts of the play recited by the narrator (in keeping with the tradition of the puppet theater), generally embellished by the dramatist with his most poetic language, are relatively free of ornamentation. Ikku commented, "This play is written throughout in a style that avoids lengthy speeches and keeps the expression as terse as possible. The style consequently differs greatly from that of Chikamatsu Monzaemon. It generally avoids poetic language or quotations from Japanese and Chinese texts, and states only what is essential. That is why one never tires of seeing it." [13]

There are splendid scenes for each of the characters, but the play stands or falls with Yuranosuke. His breathless arrival at the very moment of Enya's *seppuku* was brilliantly conceived. Ikku described how the scene came to be written:

This act was written by the dramatist Senryū. At first he had difficulties with Yuranosuke's entrance. This is the central character of the play, and his first appearance is therefore crucial. Yuranosuke has rushed from the country to his master's side, not wasting a moment, just as soon as he learned of the troubles. Senryū felt nevertheless that it would seem precipitous and undignified if Yuranosuke came bursting pell-mell onto the scene. On the other hand, it would not be appropriate to have Yuranosuke make his entrance with a serene, self-possessed expression on his face. At a loss what to do, Senryū consulted Takeda Izumo, who said, "You haven't hit on the right formula because you've been considering both possibilities. But think— Yuranosuke has raced to the scene, without pausing day or night. Presumably he has already heard that the government has

13 *Ibid.*, p. 453.

sent an official with an order commanding Hangan to commit *seppuku* that day. You must find some way to show Yuranosuke in a state of bewilderment and agitation quite unlike his usual self-possession." Senryū accordingly hit on the idea of having Yuranosuke rush up at the precise instant when Hangan, turning the point of his dagger towards himself, plunges it into the right side of his abdomen. This created a most ingenious effect.[14]

From the moment of this superb entrance Yuranosuke is unmistakably the hero of the play, and his particular virtue, loyalty, is its theme. But although Yuranosuke's presence is felt throughout the rest of the play, only in the seventh act is he the chief figure. This act clearly seems the high point of the work, though Ikku, for all the astuteness of his other judgments, preferred the elaborately contrived ninth act.

The great scene at the Ichiriki Teahouse opens with two loyal samurai arriving with the intention of discussing with Yuranosuke plans for the vendetta. One of them says, "At first I thought it was some trick of his to throw the enemy off the scent. But he has abandoned himself to his pleasures more than convincingly. I simply don't understand it." When Yuranosuke appears the two samurai ask when the conspirators are to set off for Kamakura, but he puts them off with a foolish song. Next, Heiemon, a low-ranking samurai, describes his valiant efforts to gain admittance to the league. Yuranosuke twits him: "It's quite true that I felt a certain amount of indignation—about as big as a flea's head split by a hatchet—and tried forming a league of forty or fifty men, but what a crazy notion that was!" He ends up with the cry, "Oh, when I hear the samisens playing like that I can't resist!" The loyal samurai leave, dismayed and disgusted.

[14] *Ibid.*, pp. 442–43.

So far we ourselves are not sure whether these antics are feigned or Yuranosuke has in fact surrendered himself to the pleasures of the licensed quarters. But then Rikiya, his son, arrives. He goes up to the room where his father lies, apparently in a drunken stupor, and clinks the hilt of his sword against the scabbard. At once Yuranosuke is awake and totally sober. He accepts the letter from Lady Kaoyo and sends Rikiya away.

Immediately afterwards the villainous Kudayū appears. At once Yuranosuke assumes a different guise, that of the jovial reprobate. Kudayū challenges him:

KUDAYŪ: There's no point in pretending, Yuranosuke. Your dissipation is, in fact—

YURANOSUKE: You think it's a trick to enable me to attack the enemy?

KUDAYŪ: Of course I do.

YURANOSUKE: How you flatter me! I thought you'd laugh at me as a fool, a madman—over forty and still a slave to physical pleasure. But you tell me it's all a scheme to attack the enemy! Thank you, good Kudayū. You've made me happy.

Kudayū tests Yuranosuke by offering him some octopus to eat with his saké. Yuranosuke cheerfully accepts a piece. Kudayū reminds him that the next day is the anniversary of Enya Hangan's death, and that it is considered especially important to refrain from eating animal food on the night before. He asks, "Are you going to eat that octopus and think nothing of it?" Yuranosuke replies, "Of course I'll eat it. Or have you had word that Lord Enya has turned into an octopus?"

Yuranosuke staggers off to join the women in the next

room. He forgets his sword, unthinkable in a samurai. Kudayū examines it, and discovers that the blade is rusty "as a red sardine." He leaves, more or less reassured that Yuranosuke is harmless. But he is still worried about the letter he saw Rikiya deliver, and he hides under the verandah to observe Yuranosuke further.

Yuranosuke returns, singing, but once he is sure he is alone he breaks off the song and opens the letter scroll. He reads, letting the scroll hang down over the edge of the veranda, where Kudayū eagerly peruses it. At the same time, Okaru, in a second-story room across the way, is also reading, curious about the contents of what she supposes is a love letter. An ornament falls from Okaru's hair. The sound startles Yuranosuke and he hides the letter. At once he changes again. This time he flirts with Okaru, pretending to be in love. He exchanges some rather obscene jokes with her before he finally proposes marriage. He leaves to get the money needed for her "ransom."

Heiemon, Okaru's brother, appears and quickly apprises her of the meaning of Yuranosuke's gesture. She decides that she must kill herself, but Yuranosuke returns in time to prevent her suicide. His attitude is magnanimous as he praises the loyalty of brother and sister. Then he goes back to the room where he read the letter and suddenly drives his sword through the floor, stabbing Kudayū hiding below.

In this one act Yuranosuke has assumed many guises, but his every motion has been governed by his sense of loyalty and his awareness of the importance of his mission. Yuranosuke is probably the greatest role in all of Japanese drama. Famous actors have confessed their inability to display adequately all the different moods required by the seventh act. The actor must, for example, somehow convey intense repug-

nance while eating the octopus, even as he banters with
Kudayū, who is intently observing his expression. Obviously,
the role is better suited to an actor than to a puppet, but
other roles—like that of Sagisaka Bannai—seem specifically
intended for puppets.

Yuranosuke's loyalty is absolute. There is nothing to suggest that he would have been a particle less loyal to Enya
Hangan even if the latter had been a cruel or contemptible
master. The "debunkers" of traditional history who have
asserted that Enya (Asano), far from being a noble samurai,
was avaricious and cruel,[15] only make us marvel all the more
at the unswerving loyalty of the forty-six rōnin. And if it is
true, as these writers claim, that Moronao (Kira), unlike
the mean Enya, was unusually generous to the peasants on
his lands, building waterworks for their benefit at his own
expense, it is further proof that the rōnin were uninterested
in anything but the claims of loyalty. This fact is deliberately
altered by adapters of Chūshingura for the films; in order to
please modern audiences they insist that Enya earned the
loyalty of his men by the sterling administration of his fief.
The whole point of the play is the unconditional nature of
loyalty.

It was a grave responsibility to be a samurai, but also a
privilege. Kampei desires nothing more than to be permitted
to join the avengers, but is rejected because he failed Enya
at a critical moment. His indulgence in a private matter, his
love affair with Okaru, when he should have been entirely
absorbed by his public duties as a samurai, cannot be for-
given; the fact that Kampei's misdeed was unintentional
does not make him any less guilty. Only by his suicide, the

[15] See, for example, Tamura Eitarō, Akō Roshi, pp. 41 ff, where Asano
is treated as a miser, driven by debts to his quarrel with Kira.

ultimate proof of fidelity, can he qualify for admission to the league. He becomes in death the forty-seventh *rōnin*. Heiemon, on the other hand, has committed no crime—in fact, he has behaved throughout with the utmost loyalty and decorum—but he is ineligible to participate in the attack even in the most humble capacity because he is an *ashigaru*, the lowest rank of samurai. He is accorded the privilege of dying like a full samurai only after giving Yuranosuke the most extreme proof of his loyalty. But Gihei, the loyal and unselfish merchant, is unable, even in the end, to win this privilege. The best the samurai avengers can do for him is to use the name of his shop as their password. Gihei's reaction is not one of indignation that, despite his exemplary services to the league, an accident of birth has deprived him of the chance to die like the others; the most he claims is recognition that, if not a samurai, he is at least a man.

The loyalty of Honzō to his master, Wakasanosuke, is no less sincere and deep than Yuranosuke's to Enya, but seems less attractive because it is tinged with prudence. In the second act he swears he will not interfere with Wakasanosuke's intention of exacting revenge from Moronao, and demonstrates, by slicing a branch from a pine tree, how Wakasanosuke should use his sword. But hardly is Wakasanosuke out of sight than Honzō sets off on his horse for Moronao's mansion, intending to persuade him by means of a bribe to treat Wakasanosuke with greater courtesy. Honzō's plan is entirely successful, and saves the life of his master, but this act of prudence and even of self-abasement is unlikely to win the audience's approbation. We cannot imagine Yuranosuke offering a bribe, even under the same circumstances. Again, when Enya has slashed Moronao, Honzō holds him back, supposing that Enya will not be punished too severely if Moronao is not actually killed. For this action Honzō incurs the hatred, not the gratitude, of the loyal league, for the forty-six *rōnin* are sure that their master would have died happier if he had enjoyed the satisfaction of killing Moronao. Honzō redeems himself at the end by contriving, in a rather implausible manner, to provoke Rikiya into killing him; by his death he atones for his prudence. Only now does he win the sympathy of the audience, even though he has gone against his duties as a samurai in giving up his life for a cause that is not his master's. Chikamatsu Hanji (1725–83), the leading dramatist of his time, defended Honzō's character. He admitted that it was improper for a samurai to be swayed by such considerations as his daughter's desire to marry the man she loves. Honzō, instead of giving up his life, should have watched over the youthful and hot-tempered Wakasanosuke, his master. But, Hanji explained, it was pointless to argue the merits of Honzō's actions; they were governed not by abstract considerations but by "truth." [16] By this he meant that even the most prudent samurai must sometimes yield to his emotions, and he should not be condemned for that reason. The conflict between the claims of *giri*, or duty, and *ninjō*, or human feelings, is a frequent subject in plays of the time. The audiences of *Chūshingura* must have found it particularly effecting when a man, hitherto moved entirely by *giri*, breaks down and yields to overpowering *ninjō*.[17] Honzō's imprudence, far from rendering him contemptible, makes him humanly attractive.

The characters in the play and their gestures have all

[16] Jippensha, p. 457.

[17] See Minamoto Ryōen, *Giri to Ninjō*, for an illuminating discussion of the meaning of these terms in different periods.

been subjected over the years to the most detailed and sometimes fanciful exegesis. When, for example, Honzō uses
Wakasanosuke's dirk to lop off a pine branch, the gesture
presumably indicates the swift, resolute action Wakasanosuke
should take with the same dirk. But the gesture has been
interpreted as an attempt to prevent Wakasanosuke from
drawing the dirk by making the blade sticky with pine resin! [18]
Even so far-fetched an interpretation has been given great
weight as the key to a whole performance. Again, there are
today two distinct Kabuki traditions concerning the meaning of *futatsudama*, a word used in the fourth act. The first,
and more commonly accepted, takes the word to mean "two
shots," and Kampei accordingly fires two shots at the boar
(only to hit Sadakurō!). The other meaning is a "double
shot," that is, a single shot with a double charge of gun-
powder. Actors who favor this interpretation [19] fire only one
shot, but it gives off an exceptionally loud bang.

Such interpretations are sincere, if excessively ingenious;
others are more sardonic. Shikitei Samba (1776–1822), a
well-known comic writer, in several works offered perversely
novel evaluations of the main characters. Kampei, he declared, was nothing but a bandit who killed for money.
Ōboshi Yuranosuke, despite all the adulation he had been
given, was an irresponsible fool. Why, knowing of Enya
Hangan's short temper, did he dally in the country, instead
of accompanying his master to Kamakura? Or why did he
unroll Lady Kaoyo's letter in a place where it was so easy
for Kudayū and Okaru to read it? And why, if he found it
so painful to eat octopus on the anniversary of his master's
death, did he go to a teahouse that night? Enya Hangan

[18] Toita, p. 131.

[19] Matsushima accepts this interpretation. See p. 164.

himself is abused by Samba, not only for his short temper and stinginess but for his inexplicable failure to arrive on time at the reception of the imperial envoy. Moronao, on the other hand, is revealed as a model of intelligence and good sense. It is true that he sent a love poem to Enya's wife, but he never went beyond this harmless gesture, so he can scarcely be accused of serious impropriety.

The hero among heroes for Shikitei Samba was Sagisaka Bannai: "Bannai is the most loyal of all the retainers in *Chūshingura*," he declares. Bannai serves his master Moronao with absolute and unwavering fidelity, cleverly suborns Kudayū to do Moronao's work, daringly penetrates deep within the enemy stronghold to root out Yuranosuke's secret plans, and even after Moronao's death bravely and loyally fights on against hopeless odds to his last breath. "*Appare chūshin!* (Hurrah for the loyal retainer!)" is Samba's admiring cry. Bannai's only fault is having made advances towards Okaru, but after all, he is a man and not made of wood.[20]

In Samba's most famous work, *Ukiyo-buro* (The up-to-date bathhouse, [1809–12]), one of the ladies in the public bath declares that if she had been Okaru she certainly would have taken Bannai in preference to Kampei. After running over the long list of Kampei's crimes and stupidities, she expresses her great admiration for Bannai: "He served his master perfectly in every respect, and in the end died fighting for him. Compared to Kampei, he was a magnificently loyal retainer." [21]

Shikitei Samba could not have been entirely serious in his contradictions of all the accepted views, but his criticism

[20] Shikitei Samba, *Chūshingura Henkichi Ron*, p. 433.

[21] Shikitei Samba, *Ukiyo-buro* (ed. Nakamura Michio), p. 154.

seems to go beyond mere frivolity to something approaching a rejection of the ideals expressed in the play.[22] At the same time, Samba's quibbling is proof of how avidly interested he and his readers were in every detail of the play. Yuranosuke, Moronao, Kampei, Bannai, and the other characters were a part of their lives, and their desire to learn more and more about them, as if they were real people whose secrets were not fully revealed in *Chūshingura*, occasioned the many revisions and expansions of the original work.

Kabuki Versions of the Play

The Kabuki version currently performed is only intermittently faithful to the 1748 text. Whole acts are often eliminated, but long passages not in the original may be performed instead. At the end of the third act, for example, the scene in which Okaru dissuades Kampei from killing himself has been replaced by a *michiyuki* (lovers' journey) first added to the text in 1833. Audiences prefer the cheerful, lyrical effects of this scene to the prolongation of the tense atmosphere of Enya's *seppuku*: as Kampei and Okaru journey to her home in the mountains they are overtaken by Bannai, but Kampei, drawing his sword, forces Bannai to flee for his life, and the lovers continue their travels.[23] Another major addition to the play is in the last act. The vendetta scene, disappointingly skimpy in the original text, is considerably augmented. Not only do the loyal forty-six *rōnin* have greater opportunities to display their prowess, but Moronao is also provided with a doughty retainer who duels with one of the *rōnin* on a bridge. The play ends with another retainer of Moronao's, overcome with admiration at the mighty deeds

22 See Matsushima, p. 207.

23 Text in Yamamoto and Gunji, *Kanadehon Chūshingura*, pp. 21–24.

of Yuranosuke and his confederates, tearfully saying good-by as the forty-six *rōnin* leave for Sengaku-ji with Moronao's head.[24]

Other changes are smaller and depend on the particular Kabuki version followed, but they generally tend to exploit the possibilities in Kabuki for spectacular stage effects. The surrender of Enya's castle, barely stated in the original text, is developed into an impressive scene, thanks to the use of the revolving stage, which shifts the scene from inside to outside the castle, and then to a spot where we see the castle from the distance. In this scene Yuranosuke, left alone, licks the blood on the dagger Enya used to kill himself, a thrilling if terrible moment that could only be comic if performed by a puppet. Yuranosuke, as a final memento of the confiscated castle, also takes a candleholder marked with Enya's crest (or, in some versions, a paper panel from the lantern).[25] Such touches, adding bits of realism and pathos to the scene, were developed by the actors during the nineteenth century.

Perhaps the most famous single contribution of an actor to the Kabuki version of the play transformed Sadakurō from an unimportant to a major role. In the original text he appears very briefly in the fourth act, siding with his father, Ono Kudayū, in the dispute among the samurai after Enya's death. In the fifth act he appears as a highwayman, dressed in a striped kimono and wearing the hood and straw sandals associated with a bandit. The part is usually still played in this manner in puppet performances, but the tradition in Kabuki is different. In 1766 the great actor Nakamura Nakazō (1736–90), having offended the staff playwright, was pun-

24 *Ibid.*, pp. 104–15.
25 See Toita, pp. 172–73.

ished by being assigned this minor part. Probably the manager expected Nakazō would refuse the assignment; he not only accepted but enormously enhanced the role. In place of the drab costume of a mountain bandit, Nakazō played Sadakurō in the tattered crested robes of a *rōnin*, and carried a frayed umbrella with a snake's-eye design. In order to emphasize the miming of the role Nakazō resorted to the extraordinary expedient of suppressing all the dialogue. His manner of performance, always followed today by Kabuki actors, is to be invisible inside a haystack when the scene opens. The old man Yoichibei stops by the haystack to count his money, and Sadakurō, thrusting out his hand, wordlessly snatches away the wallet. He emerges abruptly and, still not uttering a word, thrusts his sword into the old man. He kicks aside the dead body, returns his sword to the scabbard, then brushes the raindrops from his hair and squeezes water from the sleeves of his kimono. Only after drying himself does he open the wallet and count the money, his lips forming the words "fifty *ryō* in gold" as he finishes. He picks up his umbrella, opens it and starts to swagger off when he sees a wild boar. Frightened, he hastily shuts the umbrella and jumps back into the haystack. He waits for the boar to pass, then comes out again. He slips in the mud, and as he falls is hit by Kampei's bullets. That is the entire role of Sadakurō, but it provides an actor with such superb opportunities for miming that it is now a coveted assignment. It is an extreme instance of how Kabuki actors sometimes transformed scenes to suit their talents, even if it meant destroying the original nature of the parts.[26]

[26] For a fuller description of the role of Sadakurō, as performed by Kabuki actors, see Nakamura Nakazō, *Temae Miso* (ed. Gunji Masakatsu), pp. 38–43, and Onoe Kikugorō, *Gei*, pp. 58–61.

Reputation of the Play

Chūshingura was an immediate success. First performed as a puppet play, it was almost immediately staged by the Kabuki actors in both Osaka and Kyoto, and soon afterwards no fewer than three companies were performing it in Edo. Ever since it has continued, in one form or another, to captivate Japanese audiences, despite the changes in Japanese society and moral ideals. It has also proved of great interest even to non-Japanese audiences when performed abroad, and was probably the first work of Japanese literature to be translated. A version in colloquial Chinese was published in 1794,[27] and from 1880 translations into English, French, and German began to appear.[28] In 1915 John Masefield even made an adaptation of the story in his curious play The Faithful. Its popularity in Japan has always been such that managers of Kabuki or puppet theaters have traditionally staged it whenever in financial straits, and film companies today have followed their example. Chūshingura has also inspired many works of art, including various sets of ukiyoe prints.

Attempts have sometimes been made to characterize Japanese culture in terms of the austerity of rock and sand gardens, or of the Nō stage, or of monochrome landscapes,

[27] The Chinese translation, entitled Chung-ch'en-k'u, made by Ch'en Hung-meng from an earlier, cruder version by another man, was reprinted in Japan in 1815. Nothing is known about when the earlier translation was made or who might have done it, nor has the original Chinese edition of Chung-ch'en-k'u been found. The translation is on the whole faithful to the original, but a fair number of poems have been added, in the manner of the hua-pên style of Chinese fiction.

[28] See Japanese Literature in European Languages, pp. 39–40, for a list of translations. The oldest seems to be the one by Frederick Victor Dickins called Chiushingura: or The Loyal League, published in 1880.

but the popularity of *Chūshingura* provides strong evidence that there is another side to Japanese culture; it gives expression to the craving for excitement, color, and even violence that is the counterpart to the austere restraint and understatement more commonly held up as being "typically" Japanese. It would be hard to imagine two works for the theater more dissimilar than the Nō play *Matsukaze* and *Chūshingura*, but these two most popular plays of their respective theaters are both quintessentially Japanese, and both are masterpieces.

Chūshingura

(The Treasury of Loyal Retainers)

Act One

NARRATOR:

"The sweetest food, if left untasted,

Remains unknown, its savor wasted." [1]

The same holds true of a country at peace: the loyalty and courage of its fine soldiers remain hidden, but the stars, though invisible by day, at night reveal themselves, scattered over the firmament. Here we shall describe such an instance, a chronicle told in simple language of an age when the land was at peace. The time is the end of the second moon of the first year of the Ryakuō era.[2] The Ashikaga shogun, Lord Takauji, having destroyed Nitta Yoshisada in battle,[3] has built himself a palace in Kyoto. His virtuous rule extends in all four directions, and the people, like grass before the wind, bend in obedience. His authority spreads its triumphant wings over the land, even to

[1] A paraphrase of a statement in the Chinese classic Li Chi.

[2] Corresponds to the end of March, 1338. However, there is a mistake in historical fact here, since the Ryakuō era did not begin until the end of the eighth moon of that year.

[3] Nitta Yoshisada (1331–38) was killed in August, 1338. (See George Sansom, A History of Japan, 1334–1615, p. 64.) There is a mistake in chronology: Nitta was still alive when the play supposedly begins.

29

Tsurugaoka,[4] where he has erected a shrine to Hachiman. To celebrate its completion his younger brother, Lord Ashikaga Tadayoshi,[5] chief of the Board of War, has journeyed to Kamakura from the capital to serve as Takauji's deputy. The governor of Kamakura, Kō no Moronao,[6] the lord of Musashi, seated below him, casts haughty and contemptuous glances around him. The officers charged with entertaining the deputy are Wakasanosuke Yasuchika, the younger brother of the Momonoi who is the lord of Harima, and Enya Hangan Takasada, the lord of the castle of Hōki. They sit impressively in the curtained enclosure before the shrine.

TADAYOSHI: Moronao—this chest contains the helmet the Emperor Godaigo bestowed on Nitta Yoshisada, the helmet Yoshisada wore in battle when he was killed by my brother Takauji. He was our enemy, but he was nonetheless a direct descendant of the Seiwa Genji,[7] and we cannot allow his helmet to lie neglected, even if he himself discarded it. My brother has solemnly commanded that we install it here in the treasury of this shrine.

NARRATOR: The lord of Musashi listens respectfully.

MORONAO: This in indeed a surprising decision by his lordship. Why should we honor the helmet Nitta wore simply

---

[4] An important Shinto shrine. The name Tsurugaoka contains the word *tsuru* (crane), occasioning a play on "wings."

[5] Tadayoshi (1306–52) was a younger half-brother of Ashikaga Takauji, the first shogun of the Muromachi line. He was a fierce and possibly demented man, not at all like the mild-mannered nobleman here portrayed.

[6] Kō no Moronao (d. 1351) was the chief lieutenant of Ashikaga Takauji.

[7] Descendants of the Emperor Seiwa (ruled 858–76) who took the surname of Minamoto.

because he was a descendant of the Seiwa? There are any number of great and minor nobles serving loyally under his lordship's banner who are also of the Seiwa Genji clan. It would be improper to enshrine Nitta's helmet.

NARRATOR: He offers his opinion without hesitation.

WAKASANOSUKE: Surely that is not the case. In my opinion, this can only be a stratagem on Lord Takauji's part. I venture to suggest that this is his way of inducing any surviving supporters of Nitta to surrender of their own accord, out of admiration for his generous gesture. Your conclusion that this plan will serve no useful purpose is too hasty.

NARRATOR: Moronao does not let him finish.

MORONAO: What presumption to call me, Moronao, too hasty! When Yoshisada was killed he was desperately fighting, but he wore no helmet. Forty-seven helmets were found scattered around his body. Who can tell which one was his? What a disgrace it would be if we enshrined some helmet, supposing it was Yoshisada's, only to discover later that we had been mistaken! Nobody has asked for advice from a young greenhorn like yourself! Remember your place!

NARRATOR: So sure is he of his lordship's favor that he pounds in his abuse arrogantly, unconcerned that he may be exposing himself to attack. Stung by the rebuke, Wakasanosuke glares at him. Enya notices the look in his eyes.

ENYA: Lord Moronao's judgments are sound, but the plan Lord Momonoi has suggested is well-suited to times of peace, and we cannot disregard it. Let us look for guidance from the wisdom of Lord Tadayoshi, who is a master of the arts of both war and peace.

NARRATOR: Tadayoshi looks pleased at these words.

TADAYOSHI: I anticipated you would say as much and, having a plan of my own, I have given orders that Enya's wife be brought here. Invite her into our presence.

NARRATOR: There is an answering shout of obedience. Presently Lady Kaoyo, the wife of Enya, enters. She is barefoot [8] and her trailing robes brush with their hems, like the sacred brooms, the white sand of the approach to the shrine. Her lightly powdered face is of jewel-like beauty. She kneels at a respectful distance and bows.

Moronao, a great fancier of women, calls to her from where he sits.

MORONAO: Lady Kaoyo, honored consort of Lord Enya, you must be fatigued from your long waiting. His Excellency has summoned you. Please come nearer.

NARRATOR: His expression is gracious. Tadayoshi, seeing her, speaks.

TADAYOSHI: I shall tell you why I have summoned you. The Emperor Godaigo bestowed on Yoshisada the helmet which he himself had worn in the capital at the time of the Genkō uprising.[9] It is quite certain therefore that Yoshisada would have worn it in his last hours, but no one here can recognize this helmet. I have heard that at the time, Lady Kaoyo, you were one of the twelve maids of honor in the palace and were in charge of the armory. I am sure that you must have been familiar with the helmet. If you can remember which it is, identify for us, as an expert, the authentic helmet.

NARRATOR: Even this stern command is gently spoken, for it is addressed to a woman. Her answer too is soft.

[8] Going barefoot was a sign of deference.

[9] The name given to the ill-fated attempt of the Emperor Godaigo to wrest power from the Kamakura shogunate in 1331.

KAOYO: I am unworthy of your gracious command. That helmet, the one the emperor wore, I have often held in my hands, and when Lord Yoshisada received it, it was I who took the helmet from the emperor and gave it to him, together with the rare incense called Ranjatai.[10] Yoshisada said, on receiving the gift, "Man lasts but one lifetime, his name for all eternity. When the time comes for me to die in battle, I shall burn enough of this Ranjatai inside the helmet to leave its fragrance on my hair when I wear it. If, then, someone reports he has taken a head that smells of a rare incense, you will know that Yoshisada has met his end." I cannot imagine that he acted otherwise than he promised.

NARRATOR: Moronao, who has designs on Kaoyo, listens with dilated nostrils, hanging on her words. Tadayoshi has heard her attentively.

TADAYOSHI: Kaoyo's answer leaves nothing in doubt. I thought this would be the case, and I therefore had the forty-seven helmets placed in this chest. Examine them, Kaoyo, and choose the right one.

NARRATOR: At his command some samurai of lower rank, crouching deferentially, unfasten the bent curve of the lock. Kaoyo approaches, unhesitant and unafraid, impatient for the helmets to be produced. Now she sees the star-crested helmets for which Kamakura Mountain is famous,[11] acorn helmets, lion-head helmets, and ensigns marked in the styles of the different schools. And again,

[10] A celebrated perfumed wood, kept at the Tōdaiji in Nara in the Shōsōin. It is believed to have been imported from China in the eighth century.

[11] There is an allusion here to an old poem about the joy of a traveler who had the moon and stars to illumine his path over Kamakura Mountain.

there are flat-crowned, vertical-striped helmets, and helmets without flaps, for ease in drawing the bow. Among all these helmets, each fashioned to its owner's taste, is one with five flaps and a dragon's head. Before she can say, "This is the one!" they all catch the scent of rare perfume.

KAOYO: This is Yoshisada's helmet, the one I knew.

NARRATOR: She holds it out. Tadayoshi accepts her judgment.

TADAYOSHI: Enya and Momonoi, you are to place this helmet in the treasury. Come with me.

NARRATOR: He rises from his seat and, dismissing Kaoyo, goes up the steps to the shrine. Enya and Momonoi accompany him within. Kaoyo, having nothing further to detain her, prepares to leave.

KAOYO: Lord Moronao, you have duties to perform, tedious though they may be, which will require your presence here somewhat longer. Please make yourself comfortable while waiting. But I dare not remain any longer, now that I have been dismissed. I take my leave.

NARRATOR: But as she rises, Moronao sidles up to her and suddenly catches her sleeve.

MORONAO: Wait, please wait a moment. I have something I intended to take to your house and show you as soon as I had finished my duties today. Fortunately, however, you were summoned here. Lord Tadayoshi is the god who has brought us together. As you know, I am devoted to the art of poetry and have asked Yoshida no Kenkō to be my teacher.[12] We correspond daily. This is a letter of enquiry he asked me to deliver to you. I hope that your answer will be "Yes." Feel free to tell me from your own lips.

NARRATOR: He slips from his sleeve to hers a letter folded into a knot. She is astonished to see the superscription; "To the

[12] Kenkō was indeed Kō no Moronao's teacher of poetry, but probably at a later date than 1338. See my translation, *Essays in Idleness*, p. xv.

lady whose cruelty belies her beauty. From her Musashi suitor." She wonders, should she brusquely put him to shame? But that would only cause her husband's name to figure in gossip. Should she take the letter home and show it to her husband? No—in that case Lord Enya might give way to feelings of outrage and this might lead to injury or some other mishap. So, without saying a word, she casts back the letter in Moronao's direction. He picks it up, anxious lest someone else should see it.

MORONAO:

> When I realize
> She has touched it with her hand,
> If only to spurn it,
> I cannot discard it now,
> This letter I myself wrote.[13]

I shall not bore you with long explanations, but I assure you that I shall continue to press my suit again and again, until I have a favorable reply. I, Moronao, can make the country rise or fall at my pleasure; and whether I let Enya live or kill him depends on your heart, Kaoyo, alone. Don't you see this is so?

NARRATOR: Kaoyo has no reply but her tears. At this moment Wakasanosuke happens to pass. He at once perceives that Moronao has been behaving outrageously, in his usual manner.

WAKASANOSUKE: Haven't you left yet, Lady Kaoyo? Delaying here after you've been dismissed risks offending His Excellency. I suggest you leave at once.

NARRATOR: When Wakasanosuke urges her to depart Kō no Moronao thinks, "He suspects something," but he is determined not to reveal his weakness.

[13] This poem, in a slightly different version, is given in *Taiheiki* in the chapter "Slander and Death of Enya Hangan."

MORONAO: Is this more of your uncalled-for meddling? I'll tell her to leave when the time comes for her to leave. Kaoyo has requested me to make sure that her husband performs his official duties properly on this great occasion, precisely what one would expect of Enya's wife. That's true even of a daimyo, and as for you, a minor flunky, your stipend is so small you might just as well throw it away, but do you know whom you have to thank for it? Your position is so precarious one word from me could reduce you to carrying a beggar's bowl. And to think you consider yourself a samurai!

NARRATOR: He abuses Wakasanosuke in revenge for having been interfered with. Wakasanosuke, enraged, clutches the hilt of his sword so fiercely he almost crushes it; remembering, however, he is in the presence of the gods and of His Excellency, he manages this time to restrain himself. But one more harsh word from Moronao and a life and death combat would have ensued. Just then the voices of heralds proclaim the return of His Excellency, clearing the way. Wakasanosuke has no choice but to put off his revenge, yet he will not forget the indignation in his heart. Kō no Moronao's luck holds strong, and he escapes death, despite his evil actions. Now Enya enters, bringing up the rear of the procession, quite unaware that tomorrow Moronao will be his deadly enemy. Lord Tadayoshi walks with serene dignity and his majestic demeanor suggests the dragon frontlet of the helmet enshrined in the treasury. Each of the helmets has been marked with one of the forty-seven letters of the syllabary. But Tadayoshi, in place of a metal helmet, wears a silken hood, untorn like this well-ordered country, whose rule will last forever.

Act Two

NARRATOR: At the hour of dusk on an April day the grounds of the mansion of Momonoi Wakasanosuke Yasuchika are ceremoniously swept. The chief retainer, who guards the mansion as the pine in the garden has watched over it for thousands of generations, is Kakogawa Honzō Yukikuni, a man of fifty years, at the height of his powers. Attired in a stiffly creased kimono, he walks outside the reception room of the mansion. The servants sweeping the grounds are unaware of his presence.

BEKUSUKE: What do you say, Sekinai? Hasn't his lordship been making tremendous preparations these past few days? Yesterday his guests from the capital paid a formal visit to the Hachiman at Tsurugaoka. That meant a terrific outlay. I wish I had the money he spent. If I had that much money I'd change my name from Bekusuke and enjoy myself.

SEKINAI: What do you mean, you'd change your name and enjoy yourself? That's a new one. What would you change your name to?

BEKUSUKE: I'd try changing it to Kakusuke and opening a gambling joint.[14]

SEKINAI: What a lunatic! Haven't you heard what's happened? It seems our master ran into some terrible trouble at Tsurugaoka yesterday. I don't know exactly what happened, but there are rumors in the servants' quarters that Lord Moronao humiliated him in some terrible way. He must have come out with some unreasonable demand again and driven our master into a corner.

NARRATOR: They amuse themselves with foolish gossip.

HONZŌ: What's all this noisy chatter about his lordship? Do you think I would let anything go by unnoticed if it were going to bring shame on the household, especially now, when her ladyship is ill? Trouble never arises if servants know their places. If you have done with your sweeping, be off with you, all of you.

NARRATOR: His tone is mild. A maid servant brings him tobacco and he blows rings and clouds of smoke. Along the corridor a fragrance of silk is wafted as Konami, Honzō's beloved daughter, gracefully steps forth, accompanied by her mother, Tonase.

HONZŌ: Why are you here? Are you deserting her ladyship to indulge in your own pleasures? What an incredible breach of decorum!

KONAMI: No, father. Her ladyship has been in exceptionally good spirits today, and now she is sleeping quietly. That's so, isn't it, mother?

TONASE: But you know, Honzō, her ladyship was saying a while ago she had heard a rumor that yesterday, while

---

[14] *Kaku* was a slang word for one quarter of a *ryō*; the name Kakusuke, which includes this word for money, would be suitable for a banker at a gambling joint.

Konami was on her way back from Tsurugaoka, which she visited in her ladyship's place, his lordship exchanged harsh words with Lord Kō no Moronao. Her ladyship somehow got word of this, though no one informed her directly, and she is extremely upset. She asked me if my husband, who surely knows the particulars, intends to keep it a secret from her. I asked Konami, but she knew no more about what happened than I did. If something took place that will aggravate her ladyship's illness or bring disgrace on this house—

HONZŌ: But Tonase, why couldn't you have thought up some sort of answer? You know our master has a naturally short-tempered disposition. Women and children always make a big fuss over quarrels, but a samurai may have to pay for it with his life if he's made a slip of the tongue—even if it's only a word or merely half a word. You're a samurai's wife, aren't you? Couldn't you tell what to say in such a case? Be more careful in the future! (*To Konami.*) Now tell me, daughter, did you or did you not hear any rumors about this matter on your way from the shrine? No? I thought as much. (*Laughs.*) What a fuss over nothing! Very well. I myself shall go visit her ladyship directly and set her mind at ease.

NARRATOR: As he rises, a duty officer enters and announces.

OFFICER: Ōboshi Rikiya, the son of Ōboshi Yuranosuke, is here.

HONZŌ: He's probably come on Lord Hangan's behalf to discuss arrangements for entertaining our guests. Please show him in.—Tonase, listen to his message and transmit it to his lordship. The messenger is Rikiya, our daughter's fiancé and our future son-in-law. Entertain him suitably. In the meantime I shall visit her ladyship.

NARRATOR: With these parting words he goes within.

Tonase motions her daughter to her.

TONASE: Konami, it's your father's way to be strait-laced, but I thought surely he would ask *you* to receive the messenger. Instead, he asked me. His way of thinking is quite unlike your mother's! I'm sure you'd like to see Rikiya and be with him. Go and meet him in my place. Or would you rather not?

NARRATOR: Her mother repeats the question, but Konami answers neither yes nor no. Her blushes reveal her girlish innocence. Her mother, divining what is in her daughter's heart, suddenly moans.

TONASE: Oh, it hurts! Konami, press my back.

KONAMI: What's the matter?

NARRATOR: She cries out in alarm and bewilderment.

TONASE: All these worries since this morning have brought on my old complaint. I can't possibly meet the messenger in this state. Oh, oh, this pain! I'm sorry to bother you, Konami, but please listen to his report and entertain him. There's no getting the better of a master or a chronic complaint.[15]

NARRATOR: She slowly rises to her feet.

TONASE: Entertain him hospitably, Konami, but not so excessively you forget an important message. I'd also like to see my future son-in-law, but oh, this pain—

NARRATOR: Such clever use of her wits is worthy of the wife of a senior retainer. As she goes inside, Konami bows after her in appreciation.

KONAMI: I'm so grateful to you, Mother. I always long for Rikiya and miss him, but now that I'm about to see him, what am I to say?

[15] A proverb.

NARRATOR: Her maiden heart beats faster, and a tremor of expectation surges in her breast.

Ōboshi Rikiya enters, faithfully observant of the old traditions, even in his manner of walking on the *tatami*. He is not seventeen, and his forelock is combed back at an angle. So noble and clean-cut is his figure as he stands there, wearing a kimono dyed with the double whirl of his family crest [16] and a great and short sword at his sides, that he truly appears a worthy son of Ōboshi Yuranosuke. He quietly seats himself and politely inquires.

RIKIYA: Whom may I ask to transmit my message?

NARRATOR: Konami, confused, touches her hands to the floor, and they look at each other, face to face. Each loves the other deep in his heart, but is powerless to speak; their blushes, like plum and cherry blossoms, join in a contest of flowers, though no referee will award a decision in this bout of love. Konami at length quiets her agitation.

KONAMI: It was most kind of you to take the trouble to come. I have been asked to accept your message. Please transmit your words directly from your mouth to mine.

NARRATOR: She draws closer to him, but he moves away.

RIKIYA: That would be a serious breach of decorum. The most important thing in delivering or receiving a message is to observe the proper etiquette.

NARRATOR: He slides back along the *tatami* and touches his hands to the floor.

RIKIYA: This is the message my master, Enya Hangan, sends to his lordship Wakasanosuke. "Tomorrow morning before daybreak we are to wait on the shogun's deputy, Lord Tadayoshi. No doubt the guests will also arrive early. Lord

[16] The crest used by the Ōboshi family in the play was actually that of the puppet operator Yoshida Bunzaburō.

Moronao has commanded that both Hangan and Wakasanosuke report without fail at the palace by four in the
morning." My master, Hangan, ordered me to come here
as his messenger to ensure there would be no possible mis-
understanding. I request you to report what I have said
to Lord Wakasanosuke.

NARRATOR: Kanomi is so enraptured by his face as he fluently
recites the message that she fails even to respond.

WAKASANOSUKE: I have heard everything. I thank you, messenger, for your trouble.

NARRATOR: Wakasanosuke emerges from the inner room.

WAKASANOSUKE: I unfortunately have not had the opportunity to see Lord Hangan since we parted yesterday. Yes, I
will certainly meet him at four tomorrow morning. I understand the matter perfectly. Please express my gratitude
to Lord Hangan for his pains and convey to him my
compliments. I am much obliged to you too.

RIKIYA: Then, sir, I shall be taking my leave. (*To Konami.*)
Thank you, lady, for hearing my message.

NARRATOR: He composedly rises to his feet and, without so
much as a backward glance, straightens the lapels of his
kimono and departs.

    Honzō enters at the same moment.

HONZŌ: I did not realize you were here, your lordship. Tomorrow morning you are to be present at the palace at
four. It is now already close to midnight. I suggest you
rest for a while.

WAKASANOSUKE: I understand, Honzō, but I have a little
business with you first, a private matter. Please send
Konami inside.

HONZŌ: Konami, if we have any need of you we will clap our
hands. Go inside now.

NARRATOR: He dismisses his daughter; then, uncertain of the

meaning of the expression on his master's face, he goes
up to him.

HONZŌ: I have been intending to ask you, my lord, what
happened. Please tell me everything.

NARRATOR: As he edges towards him the master also draws
closer.

WAKASANOSUKE: Honzō, I want you to swear you will do
exactly as I say, no matter what it is, and not attempt to
dissuade me.

HONZŌ: Your words have a solemn ring, your lordship. Of
course I will obey you, but—

WAKASANOSUKE: You mean you can't give me your word as a
samurai?

HONZŌ: That is not so. But first I should like to hear the full
details.

WAKASANOSUKE: You'd have me tell you everything and afterwards remonstrate?

HONZŌ: No, I mean—

WAKASANOSUKE: You'll disobey me? What do you say?

NARRATOR: Honzō looks down, dismayed. For a while he remains silent but, steeling his resolution, he at length draws
his dagger with one hand and with the other slips out his
sword. He strikes metal against metal.[17]

HONZŌ: Now you know my intentions. I will not seek to stop
you, nor reveal your secret to anyone. But I beg you to
disclose what you have in mind, slowly and carefully, so
that even a fool like myself can understand completely.

WAKASANOSUKE: Very well, I'll tell you. Ashikaga Tadayoshi,
the shogun's deputy, has deigned to travel down to Kama-

[17] The striking together of the dagger and sword was a common
manner used in swearing an oath by a samurai; it implied that if he
broke his oath he would never again be able to wear a sword as a
samurai.

kura for the consecration of the shrine at Tsurugaoka. Enya Hangan and I have been charged with entertaining him. By further command of the Shogun Takauji, Kō no Moronao was appointed our adviser, and we have been directed to obey his instructions in everything concerning the entertainment. We have followed this command in deference to Moronao's age and his being a samurai of wide experience. But his head is so swollen by the honor that he is acting ten times more arrogantly than usual. In the presence of the assembled samurai from the capital he abused and railed at me, singling me out because of my youth. I was ready to slash him in two but, out of respect for the shogun's command, I time and time again restrained myself. Tomorrow I will not bear it any longer. I will display my mettle as a samurai by putting him to shame before His Excellency, and then cutting him down. Under no circumstances are you to interfere. My wife always calls me short-tempered, and you too have remonstrated with me. I have recognized this failing of mine again and again, but think what it does to a soldier's spirit to have this frustrated rage keep accumulating inside him. I am not unaware that this will bring extinction to my household and despair to my wife, but as a samurai I owe the service of my sword to the god of war. I shall not be dying on the field of battle, but if I can kill that one man, Moronao, it will benefit the nation. That is more important than the disgrace to my family. I am sure people will say of me that Wakasanosuke ruined his life because of his short temper, and that he was a reckless and turbulent samurai. That is why I have told you the whole story.

NARRATOR: He yields to tears of impotent rage, torn by a pain that shoots through his entrails. Honzō claps his hands.

HONZŌ: How admirable! Thank you for your explanation. How splendid to have endured such provocation! If I had been in your place, I could not have stood it so long.

WAKASANOSUKE: What do you mean, Honzō? Do you look down on me for having put up with so much and been so patient?

HONZŌ: Those words do not sound like you, sir. The townspeople have a proverb, that if you keep to the shady side of the street in winter and to the sunny side in summer, steering clear of people on the way, you'll be as safe as in your own back yard, for there's no danger of a quarrel or argument with anyone crossing your path. But a samurai cannot regulate himself by such devious conduct. Am I mistaken, fool that I am, in thinking that there is no limit to what people will demand if you yield the road to them? Here, I'll show you my true feelings. I'll prove how seriously I take your words.

NARRATOR: He takes the dirk lying beside his lordship and unsheathes it. The next instant he snatches up with one hand a straw sandal from the step, and swiftly folding it, strops the blade. Suddenly he slashes through a branch of the pine before the veranda, then deftly slips the dirk back into its scabbard.

HONZŌ: My lord, act decisively, as I have done!

WAKASANOSUKE: I hardly needed reminding.—But someone may be listening.

NARRATOR: They look around them.

HONZŌ: It is still only one o'clock. There is time yet for a good rest. I'll see to it myself that the alarm clock by your pillow is set. Hurry, you need the sleep.

WAKASANOSUKE: I'm glad you have agreed. I'll go now to my wife and say goodbye, as casually as I can. I shall not see you again, Honzō. Farewell.

NARRATOR: With these parting words he goes inside. A samurai's spirit allows no compromise.

Honzō, having watched his master leave, runs to the back gate.

HONZŌ: Where are Honzō's men? Bring my horse at once!

NARRATOR: Before he has even finished speaking, the men lead the horse into the garden. Honzō girds himself and leaps from the veranda onto the horse's back.

HONZŌ: To Moronao's mansion! Follow me!

NARRATOR: As he rides out, Tonase and Konami rush up and cling to the horse's reins.

TONASE: Where are you going? We've heard everything. Why couldn't you have used the wisdom of your years to dissuade our master, Honzō? I can't understand you. I won't let you go.

NARRATOR: Mother and daughter hang onto the bridle, holding him back.

HONZŌ: What brazen impudence! I've done what I have because of my concern for our master's life and the reputation of his house. I forbid you to say a word of this to his lordship. If he hears of it, I'll disinherit you, Konami, and break up our marriage, Tonase. Now, men, I'll give you your orders on the way. Out of my way, both of you!

WOMEN: No, no—

HONZŌ: Blasted nuisance!

NARRATOR: He aims a kick with the point of his stirrup. It strikes squarely, and the women, moaning, topple over. He does not so much as look at them.

HONZŌ: Follow me, men.

NARRATOR: He digs in his knees and the horse, kicking up the dust, gallops out of sight.

Act Three

NARRATOR: Lord Ashikaga Tadayoshi, the shogun's deputy for the Eight Eastern Provinces, has recently built himself a magnificent palace, and here the great and minor lords in their lavishly ornamented robes of state are arrayed, sleeve against sleeve, brilliant as the stars and moon at night over Kamakura Mountain. The Nō actors who will take part in the entertainment enter by the back gate and the guests by the front gate. The officers charged with the banqueting arrive at the palace promptly at four. The glory of the samurai shines in full radiance.

From the watchtower of the western gate, preceded by flashing lanterns, the governor of Musashi, Kō no Moronao, enters imposingly, his head held high in token of his power. He wears a pale-blue crested robe and a court cap that nods proudly, like the arrogance in his heart. Moronao has left his retainers at the different samurai stations, and only a few menials clear the way before him. Wearing the borrowed dignity of his master, Sagisaka Bannai swaggers in, aping his betters.[18]

[18] The name Sagisaka contains the word *sagi* (heron), and there are numerous plays on words associated with it. Here the text says literally, "a heron that imitates a crane."

BANNAI: Excuse me for saying so, master, but you acquitted yourself nobly today before the shogun. Men like Enya or Momonoi are aways giving themselves airs, but when it comes to etiquette and ceremony they're helpless as a dog thrown up on the roof. Why, it's enough to put you in stitches. Which reminds me, I hope you're not upset that Enya's wife Kaoyo still hasn't sent you an answer. She's a good-looking woman, but she's not my type. There's no comparison between a man like Enya and you, Lord Moronao, who stand first in His Excellency's confidence.

MORONAO: Don't talk so loud! Kaoyo is faithful to her husband. I have tried repeatedly to make love to her, under the pretext of giving her poetry lessons, but still she won't consent. I gather she has a new maid, Karu by name. I intend to suborn her and get her to do my bidding. I still have a few tricks up my sleeve. If Kaoyo really disliked me she would certainly have blabbed the whole thing to her husband. The fact that she hasn't gives me some hope.

NARRATOR: As master and retainer, standing beneath the four-pillared gate, chat together, nodding their heads in agreement, a samurai on guard at the watchtower rushes in excitedly.

SAMURAI: We were on duty in the guardroom at the watchtower when Kakogawa Honzō, a retainer of Momonoi Wakasanosuke, came up. He said he had gone to your mansion on horseback, hoping to have a personal audience with you, but you had already left for the palace. He says he must see you at all costs, and has brought a lot of retainers with him. What answer shall I give him?

NARRATOR: Bannai flies into a fury at the words.

BANNAI: The gall of him, asking for an audience with Lord

Moronao, just today when his lordship's so busy! I'll see him myself.

NARRATOR: He starts to run out.

MORONAO: Wait! Control yourself, Bannai! It's plain what he's come for. His master wants to settle his grudge over what happened the day before yesterday at Tsurugaoka, but instead of challenging me himself, he's sent this Honzō, hoping to humiliate me. . . . Ha, ha. Keep your wits about you, Bannai. We've still some time before the ceremony. Call him here. I'll take care of him.

BANNAI: Oh, I see now. Men, be on your guard!

NARRATOR: Master and retainer wet the rivets of their swords [19] and wait, eager and ready for a fight.

Kakogawa Honzō, at a word from Moronao, composedly enters his presence, every fold of his garments neatly ordered. He directs his servants to arrange before Moronao the gifts they have brought; then, respectfully withdrawing to a distance, kneels before him.

HONZŌ: I make bold to address myself to you, Lord Moronao. My master, Wakasanosuke, has been designated by the Shogun Takauji to perform on this occasion an important office. This is an honor to him as a samurai, and a stroke of good fortune beyond his deserts. Wakasanosuke, being young and untutored in matters of ceremonial, was worried about what might happen, but because you, Lord Moronao, have condescended to instruct and guide him in all things, he has been able to discharge his duties successfully. My master in no way deserves credit for this—it is entirely thanks to your kind intercession, Lord Moronao. What

---

[19] They wet the rivet with saliva to keep it from flying from the handle when the sword is drawn.

greater joy could there be for my master and mistress and all the rest of us in his household? That is why I have brought these gifts, exceedingly meager though they are. They are offered to you by the entire household, as a token of our gratitude. If your lordship will deign to accept them, you will do us the greatest honor we can know in this lifetime. I most earnestly beg you to accept. (*To Bannai.*) Here is a list of the contents. Please offer it to your master.

NARRATOR: He hands the list to Bannai, who snatches it from him and with a baffled expression opens the scroll.

BANNAI: "List of gifts. Thirty rolls of silk and thirty pieces of gold from Lady Wakasanosuke. Twenty pieces of gold from the chief retainer, Kakogawa Honzō. Ten pieces of the same from the chief of the residence guards. Ten pieces of the same from the samurai of the household. The above as enumerated."

NARRATOR: As he reads out the list Moronao stands dumfounded, his mouth gaping in astonishment. The two men exchange glances and stare around them, bewildered, like merrymakers learning that the summer festivals have all been postponed for the year.[20] Suddenly Moronao speaks, in quite altered tones.

MORONAO: This is indeed a surprise. I am most grateful for such kind attentions. What should we do, Bannai?

BANNAI: It seems to me we would be disregarding their wishes if we declined the gifts, and that would be the worst possible breach of etiquette.

MORONAO: Moments like these, even for a teacher of deco-

[20] The principal festivals in Osaka took place at the end of the sixth month; people anticipated them for months, and if they were called off because of bad weather or any other reason there would be great disappointment. Although the scene is set in Kamakura, the theater itself was in Osaka.

rum, are the most embarrassing. Master Honzō, I've given nothing worthy of the name "instructions," and in any case Lord Wakasanosuke is such a capable man he's beyond a teacher like myself. Bannai, take these gifts and put them away safely. But how rude of me—I can't even offer you a cup of tea, here on the street.

NARRATOR: Honzō, hearing these polite phrases, a complete turnabout in Moronao's manner, realizes that his stratagem has met with success, but still he keeps his hands politely touching the ground.

HONZŌ: It is four o'clock now. I must take my leave. The ceremony today is especially important, and I entreat you therefore to give my master greater guidance than ever.

NARRATOR: He starts to leave, but Moronao catches his sleeve.

MORONAO: Why are you running off? Wouldn't you like to see the ranks of nobles gathered in the palace today?

HONZŌ: I should be embarrassed, as a mere retainer, to appear before His Excellency.

MORONAO: No matter, no matter. As long as I am with you nobody will dare object. Besides, Lord Wakasanosuke may also have some service to ask of you. Stay, by all means.

NARRATOR: Honzō responds to this urging.

HONZŌ: In that case, I shall go with you. It would be rude to refuse so kind an invitation. After you, my lord.

NARRATOR: He follows Moronao out. Honzō, sure that money would win the day, has purchased even the life of his master; the faithful retainer has calculated correctly.[21] But

21 There are various untranslatable plays on words in this passage. The language is drawn from the special terms used in making calculations on an abacus. Honzō is called literally "a white rat," this animal having been a messenger of the god of good luck and therefore an appropriate symbol for a faithful retainer. The cries of the rat, *chū, chū*, lead into the word *chūgi* (loyalty).

the path of loyalty, devotion, and obedience is a straight
one, straight as the road they take through the gate.

Soon afterwards Enya Hangan Takasada enters. He too
has left his retainers behind, and has kept his palanquin
waiting outside. Hayano Kampei, whose family has served
Enya's for many generations, strides up to the throng at
the gate, wearing a new *hakama*, reddish-brown in color,
and dyed in small patterns, that rustles as he walks. He
shouts.

KAMPEI: Enya Hangan presents himself at the palace.

NARRATOR: A sentry comes forward.

SENTRY: His lordship Momonoi arrived at the palace some
time ago and inquired about your lordship. Just now Lord
Moronao also appeared and asked where you were. They
have already gone inside.

ENYA: Kampei—they've gone in already! How embarrassing
to be late!

NARRATOR: Kampei is his only attendant as he hurries inside
to His Excellency's presence.

Inside the palace the Nō chorus, entertaining the guests,
is singing the passage, "We have reached the Bay of Takasago on the Harima Coast." [22] Their chanting voices are
carried by the wind to the willow outside the gate. No less
graceful than the willow in her appearance is the young
woman of some eighteen years who comes along now, her
delicate eyebrows dark as pine boughs. Her face is shielded
by a hood, and she wears with assurance, as one trained
in a strict household, a kimono with the sash tied behind.
Her servant holds a lantern marked with the crest of the
house of Enya.

[22] The play being chanted is the felicitous *Takasago*. For this particular
passage see the translation in *Japanese Noh Drama*, I, 6.

OKARU: The day will soon be breaking. You are not allowed inside the gate. Go home and rest.

NARRATOR: The servant, with a cry of obedience, departs. The young woman peeps inside the gate.

OKARU: I wonder what Kampei is doing. There's something I must see him about.

NARRATOR: As she looks around, Kampei catches a glimpse of her from behind.

KAMPEI: Okaru—that's you, isn't it?

OKARU: Kampei, I wanted so badly to see you. I'm glad you're here.

KAMPEI: I don't understand. What are you doing here in the middle of the night, all alone, without even a servant?

OKARU: Oh, I just sent back the servant who brought me here. I've been waiting here alone because I have a message from her ladyship. She asked me to see you and give you this letter box to put in Lord Hangan's hands. And you are to relay her message to him: "Forgive me for bothering you, but please deliver this return poem with your own hand to Lord Moronao." Her ladyship, on further thought, was afraid something might go wrong, with all the crowd in the palace, and she suggested I not try tonight. But I was so anxious to see you that I assured her his lordship would have time enough to deliver a poem or two. I ran here all the way. Oh, I'm exhausted!

NARRATOR: She sighs with relief.

KAMPEI: In other words, all that has to be done is for our master to hand this letter box personally to Moronao? Very well. I'll give it to him. Wait for me. I'll be coming back.

NARRATOR: As he speaks a voice is heard from inside the gate: "Kampei, Kampei, Kampei! Lord Hangan is calling you."

KAMPEI: Yes, sir. Coming at once. (*To Okaru.*) I've got to hurry.

NARRATOR: He shakes free his sleeve and rushes off. Sagisaka Bannai tiptoes gingerly in.[23]

BANNAI: There you are, Okaru. Love certainly inspires a man with wisdom, doesn't it? When I saw you fooling with Kampei I shouted, "Kampei, your master's calling for you." Pretty clever of me, wasn't it? Lord Moronao says he's got something to ask you. And I'd like just once to take you and—oh, sweetheart!

NARRATOR: He tries to embrace her, but she pushes him away.

OKARU: Don't try to take liberties with me! What an outrageous way for someone from a household famed for its decorum to behave! What shocking impudence! What a shocking breach of conduct!

NARRATOR: Spurned by her, Bannai exclaims.

BANNAI: And what a cold-hearted woman! Here in the dark, where nobody can see, how about it?

NARRATOR: As he struggles to catch her hand, voices call.

SERVANTS: Master Bannai, you're wanted on urgent business by Lord Moronao.

NARRATOR: Two servants appear. Their eyes goggle at what they see.

SERVANTS: Good heavens, Master Bannai! Lord Moronao has been asking for you for the longest time. And here we find you with a woman in your arms, you who serve in a house known for its strict decorum! What shocking impudence! What a shocking breach of conduct!

BANNAI: Damn it—that's just what she said!

---

[23] Literally, "as if stepping on mudfish," a play on the name Sagisaka, with *sagi* used as the heron that gingerly steps on the mudfish.

NARRATOR: He puffs his cheeks with anger as he goes off with them. Kampei arrives just as Bannai is leaving.

KAMPEI: Did you see what I just did? Bannai swallowed the bait and now he's gone. If I had shown up myself and told him his master was calling for him, I'm sure he would have said, "Drop it! I've heard that one before." That wouldn't have been much fun, so I got his servants drunk instead. He can't say he's heard *that* one before! (*Laughs.*) My plan worked beautifully.

OKARU: Why not include this in your plan? Just for a minute—

NARRATOR: She takes his hand.

KAMPEI: You're really carried away, aren't you! Wait a while.

OKARU: What do you mean? What is there to wait for? It'll soon be dawn. Come on, please.

NARRATOR: He is powerless to resist, for the groundwork of love has been laid, and her suggestion suits him well.

KAMPEI: But there're so many people coming and going here.

NARRATOR: They hear inside the palace the voices of the actors intoning the passage from *Takasago;* "I approach the base of the pine and rub the trunk. . . ."

KAMPEI: That music gives me an idea. Let's sit down somewhere.

NARRATOR: Hand in hand they go off.

The first Nō play has ended, and the tuning of the hand drum and the thump of the big drum can be heard from the dressing room, in celebration of the peace and prosperity of the land. Lord Tadayoshi is in unusually good spirits.

Wakasanosuke has been waiting impatiently for Moronao. He glances at the interior of the hall, tightens the cords of his long *hakama,* and watches for some sign of

Moronao's approach, breathlessly impatient to draw his
sword and slash Moronao in two. Moronao and his retainer, unaware that Wakasanosuke is waiting for them,
catch sight of him from afar.

MORONAO: Ah, there you are, Lord Wakasanosuke. How early
you've arrived at the palace! You put me to shame. I am
most embarrassed. But speaking of embarrassment, there's
something I must explain and apologize for.

NARRATOR: He throws down his two swords.

MORONAO: Lord Wakasanosuke, I must clarify what hap-
pended. I am sure you must have been angered, and quite
justifiably so, by the intemperate language I used the
other day at Tsurugaoka. It was a temporary, inexplicable
lapse, the greatest blunder of my entire life. See, a samurai
bows before you and craves your pardon most humbly.
Fortunately for me, you are a man of the world. Imagine
what would have happened if it had been some excitable
roughneck instead—I would have been slashed in two! It's
terrifying even to think of it. To tell the truth, when I
saw you turn and go away I joined my hands in reverence
and bowed towards you, to express my gratitude at your
forbearance. Ah, when a man grows old he becomes foolish. Please make allowance for my age and forgive me. A
samurai throws down his swords and joins his hands in
supplication. I am sure you're not a man to refuse when
someone entreats you so. I apologize to you, again and
again. Bannai, join with me in begging his lordship's
pardon.

NARRATOR: Wakasanosuke, having not the least suspicion
that his money has inspired this flattery, feels the strength
go from his arms that had been tensed for combat, and he
can no longer draw his sword. At a loss what to do with

the finely sharpened blade, he looks down, his face wrapped in thought. Honzō, standing behind a brushwood fence, looks on, not so much as blinking.

MORONAO: Why do you suppose Enya is so late, Bannai? What an enormous difference there is between him and Lord Wakasanosuke! He's so lacking in breeding that he still hasn't shown his face here. And as they say, like master, like retainer—not one of his men ever notices when something has gone wrong. Come with me, Lord Wakasanosuke. We'll go together before His Excellency. Please come. Old Moronao craves your indulgence. (*To Bannai.*) Come on, you too, you paragon of intelligence.

WAKASANOSUKE: Excuse me, but I've been feeling somewhat unwell for the past few minutes. Do go ahead.

MORONAO: What's the trouble? A stomach ache? Bannai, massage his lordship's back. May I offer you some medicine?

WAKASANOSUKE: No, it's not that serious.

MORONAO: Well, then, rest here for a while. You can trust me to explain to His Excellency what has happened. Bannai, show his lordship to another room.

NARRATOR: Master and retainer shower attentions on Wakasanosuke, to his great discomfiture. Dismayed though he is, he has no choice but to retire to the next room.

HONZŌ: What a relief!

NARRATOR: He bows to the gods of heaven and earth, then withdraws to an antechamber. Soon afterwards Enya Hangan appears in the long corridor leading to the audience hall. Moronao calls out to him.

MORONAO: You're late. Late. What could you have been thinking of? Didn't I warn you in advance that the audience today would begin promptly at four o'clock?

ENYA: You are quite right. It was careless of me to have come late. But I believe there is still time before we are to appear before His Excellency.

NARRATOR: He takes the letter box from his sleeve.

ENYA: My retainer brought this just now from my wife Kaoyo with her request that I deliver it to you.

NARRATOR: He hands it to Moronao.

MORONAO: I see. Your wife, as you know, has aspirations as a poet and when she heard that I was devoted to the art of *waka* she asked me to correct her compositions. I presume that is what this letter is about.

NARRATOR: He opens it and reads.

MORONAO:

> "They would be heavy enough
> Even without this new burden,
> These night clothes.
> Do not pile onto your robes
> A robe that is not your own." [24]

This is a poem from the *New Collection*. Does she expect me to correct this old poem? Hmmm.

NARRATOR: As he ponders on the poem, it occurs to him the meaning is that his love has been rejected. He realizes too that she has probably revealed the affair to her husband. Controlling his anger, he asks casually.

MORONAO: Lord Hangan, have you seen this poem before?

HANGAN: No, this is the first time I've seen it.

MORONAO: When I was reading it? What a miraculously chaste woman you have for a wife. This poem she sent me is a typical example of her virtue. "Do not pile onto your robes a robe that is not your own." A chaste wife, yes,

[24] A poem by the priest Jakunen, no. 1964 in the *Shin Kokin Shū*. The version given here is slightly inaccurate.

chaste indeed. You're a lucky man. It's no wonder you
were late in arriving at the palace. You stick so close to
your home you can't be bothered about His Excellency.

NARRATOR: Hangan has not the least notion that Moronao
taunts him with this insinuating abuse by way of relieving
his annoyance over another matter. He is offended, but
checks his feelings.

HANGAN: Ha, ha. Very amusing. I take it, Lord Moronao,
drink has made you merry. Have you been drinking?
When was the party?

MORONAO: When would I have been drinking? Any duties I
have to perform I perform properly, even if it means re-
fusing when drink is offered me. Why were you late? Have
you been drinking? Or were you tied down by your domestic arrangements? Lord Wakasanosuke is far better
than you at his duties. Yes, your wife is a chaste woman,
a peerless beauty, and she writes a splendid hand. You
should be proud of her. But don't lose your temper.
There's not a word of untruth in what I say. Today when
His Excellency is so busy and I am busy too you choose
this particular time to say in your doting manner, "This,
sir, is a poem by my wife." If your home is so precious,
you need not come here. There's a story about a carp that
lived in a well. It applies perfectly to people like you who
stay home all the time. Listen while I tell it. This carp
thought that there was nothing in heaven and earth to
compare with his well, which was a bare three or four feet
wide, and he had never seen the outside world. One day
the well was cleaned, and they brought the carp up in a
bucket. They threw him into the river. Well, the poor
devil had always been inside a well, and it made him so
happy to be in the river that he lost his bearings and

bumped his nose against the pilings of a bridge so hard, so painfully hard, he died on the spot. You're just like that carp. Ha, ha!

NARRATOR: As he rants on, Hangan can control his rage no longer.

HANGAN: Are you out of your senses? Have you gone crazy, Moronao?

MORONAO: You wretch! How dare you call a samurai crazy, especially when he's Kō no Moronao, the first of all His Excellency's retainers!

HANGAN: Then you've meant your insults?

MORONAO: You repeat yourself. Supposing I meant what I said, what would you do about it?

HANGAN: Just this!

NARRATOR: He whips out his sword and slashes head on at Moronao, opening a great wound between the eyebrows. Moronao, shrinking back, dodges the next blow, which cuts in two the crown of his hat. Hangan prepares to strike again, but Moronao ducks and squirms away. At this moment Honzō, who has been waiting in the adjourning room, runs out and catches Hangan from behind.

HONZŌ: Lord Hangan—you've been too rash!

NARRATOR: While he holds Enya back, Moronao, stumbling and falling, makes his escape.

HANGAN: Damn you, Moronao! I'll cut you in two! Let go, Honzō, let go!

NARRATOR: Even as they struggle the mansion bursts into an uproar. Samurai of the household, the great and minor lords, all rush here and there, some subduing Hangan and wrenching away his sword, others ministering to Moronao.

The front gate and back gate are both shut, but the confusion inside the walls is apparent from the noise and the flashing of lanterns. Hayano Kampei, his eyes wild with anxiety, runs back and pounds on the back gate, violently enough to break it down. He shouts.

KAMPEI: This is Hayano Kampei, the retainer of Enya Hangan. I'm worried about my master's safety. Open up! Hurry!

NARRATOR: A loud voice answers from inside the gate.

VOICE: Go round to the front gate with your business. This is the back gate.

KAMPEI: I know it's the back gate. The front gate is jammed with a mob of household men rushing around on horseback and I can't get near. There seems to have been a fight. What happened?

VOICE: The fight's over. Enya Hangan has been confined to his residence for the crime of having attacked Lord Moronao, the first of the liegemen. He has just left in a closed palanquin.

KAMPEI: Great heavens! I must get to the mansion!

NARRATOR: He starts running.

KAMPEI: No—if his lordship is confined to his quarters, it makes it all the more hopeless for me to return to the mansion.

NARRATOR: He paces back and forth, pondering what to do. Just then the maid Okaru runs up. They had separated a few minutes before.

OKARU: Kampei, I've heard everything. What shall we do? What can we do?

NARRATOR: She clings to him, weeping, but he pushes her aside.

KAMPEI: You and your bawling face! I'm dishonored forever as a samurai. This is the end.

NARRATOR: He lays his hand on the hilt of his sword.

OKARU: Wait, I beg you. Have you lost your head, Kampei?

KAMPEI: Yes, I have. How could I help but lose my head? I was not with my master when he needed me most. On top of that, he's been sent home in a closed palanquin like a common criminal, and the gates of the mansion have closed on him. And all this time I, his retainer, was indulging in fleshly pleasures. I abandoned him. How can I show myself before people wearing my swords? Let me go this instant.

OKARU: Please wait a moment. Everything you say is true, it makes perfect sense, but who is to blame for having made a delinquent samurai of you? It was all my fault. If one of us is to die, it is I who should die before you. If you kill yourself now, who would ever praise your samurai spirit? Listen to me carefully. Come with me, for the time being, to my father's house. My father and mother are country people and you can depend on them. Just consider that what happened was ordained from a previous life, and please listen to what your wife tells you, Kampei.

NARRATOR: Words fail her, and she bursts helplessly into tears.

KAMPEI: Yes, what you say makes sense. Of course, you've only recently entered service and you couldn't possibly understand all the details of the household. The chief retainer in my master's house, Ōboshi Yuranosuke, has not yet returned from our province. I'll wait until he gets back to ask for pardon. Let us leave now, as quickly as we can.

NARRATOR: As they prepare to leave, Sagisaka Bannai rushes out with his henchmen.

BANNAI: Kampei—your master Hangan brutally attacked Lord Moronao, and as punishment for the trifling wound he inflicted, he's been confined to his house. It's obvious he'll soon have his head chopped off. (*To men.*) Twist back his arms! (*To Kampei.*) We're going to take you back and torture you to death! Prepare to meet your end!

NARRATOR: He loudly menaces Kampei.

KAMPEI: You've come at the right moment, Sagisaka Bannai. You won't make much of a meal all by yourself, but you'll see how skillfully my arm will cut you up and season you.[25]

BANNAI: Don't let him say another word, men.

MEN: Right!

NARRATOR: They fall on Kampei from both sides, but he, with a shout of "I'm ready for you!", ducks under their attack. He uses both hands to twist their arms, then kicks the men violently away from him. In their place two other men come slashing at him. He takes the blows from their swords on his scabbard. They turn round and lunge at him, but he fends them off, this time with an upward thrust of his scabbard tip and sword hilt. The four attack all at once, and now he sends them spinning off in rapid succession to right and left, as though flipping cakes on a griddle. They scatter, but in their wake Bannai furiously attacks. Kampei dodges, and grabs Bannai by the neck, then throws him head first to the ground, and sets his foot on him.

KAMPEI: You're at my mercy now. Shall I run you through or slash you? No, I'll cut you into little pieces.

NARRATOR: Okaru clings to his uplifted sword.

OKARU: If you kill him it will spoil your chances of a pardon. You've punished him enough.

---

[25] Kampei refers to Sagisaka Bannai as if he were a bird, again because of the word *sagi* (heron) in his name.

NARRATOR: She stops Kampei, and Bannai wriggles out from under his foot. Sagisaka has no feathers, but he flies for dear life.[26]

KAMPEI: I'm sorry he got away. But if I had cut him to pieces it would have been compounding disloyalty on disloyalty. For the present the two of us will go into hiding. We'll wait for the right moment to make our appeal for pardon.

NARRATOR: It is already six in the morning, and across the whitening banks of cloud to the east crows fly from their nests. *Kawai, kawai,*[27] they call, as husband and wife hurry on their way. Their hearts feel the tug of worry over the fate of their master. Such is the floating world.

[26] Another joke on the name Sagisaka, combined with an expression that means "to flee."

[27] *Kawai* represents the sound of the cawing of the crows, but it also means "dear" or "sweet" when referring to the husband and wife.

Act Four

NARRATOR: Enya Hangan is confined to his residence at Ōgigayatsu, the gates barred by great bamboo poles, and no one is allowed to enter or leave, save members of the household. The situation seems extremely grave. Even at such a time the women's quarters are gay as charming ladies-in-waiting amuse themselves. In the hope of cheering their master, the mistress of the house, Lady Kaoyo, together with Ōboshi Rikiya, has filled baskets with cherry blossoms from the Kamakura hills, double-petaled and triple-petaled, but lovelier even than the blossoms they arrange, these two lend a beauty of flowers and maple leaves to the room. Along the corridor of the Willow Chamber comes Hara Gōemon, chief of the samurai, followed by Ono Kudayū.

GŌEMON: Well, Master Rikiya, I see you've reported early for duty this morning.

RIKIYA: Not at all. I intend to remain in attendance here, day and night, until my father arrives from the country.

GŌEMON: That's admirable of you.

NARRATOR: Gōemon, impressed, touches both hands to the floor.

65

GŌEMON: How does his lordship feel today?

NARRATOR: Lady Kaoyo replies.

KAOYO: Thank you both for coming. I was worried that Lord Hangan might become depressed or even fall ill, but on the contrary, he spends the whole day gazing at the flowers blooming on the hill in the garden, and his face is cheerful. That is why I thought I might also comfort him by sending for some specially beautiful cherry blossoms and arranging them in this way.

GŌEMON: Yes, I understand what you had in mind. You intended these flowers to serve as an augury of good fortune, knowing that the nature of flowers is to open. The blossoms foretell that your gates will open and the master be released from confinement. I tried myself to think of something, but I am not very clever at such things. But let me get to the point. I've been informed that an envoy from the shogun will come here today. I'm sure he'll bring a message releasing his lordship from confinement. What do you think, Kudayū? Don't you agree?

KUDAYŪ: (*Laughs.*) Look, Gōemon. These flowers please the eyes for a moment, but as soon as the wind blows, they scatter. The same is true, exactly, of your words. It doesn't become a samurai to try to please people that way. Your words are like New Year's compliments that soon lose their sheen. Shall I tell you why? Our master was entrusted with the duty of entertaining the official guests, but instead he committed a crime, wounding the presiding officer and disturbing order in the palace. At the lightest, the sentence will be banishment, at the heaviest, *seppuku*. It was his lordship's mistake in the first place to have made an enemy of Lord Moronao.

NARRATOR: Gōemon immediately responds.

GŌEMON. Then, is it your hope that his lordship will be banished or ordered to commit *seppuku?*

KUDAYŪ: No, that's not my hope, but I believe in speaking the truth, without varnishing my words. The cause of the trouble, Gōemon, has been your stinginess. That's how it all started. If you had placated Moronao's feelings with some money, this would never have happened.

NARRATOR: The greed on his face shows he judges others by himself. Gōemon is quick to deny this.

GŌEMON: A man who fawns on another person or flatters him doesn't deserve to be called a samurai. You're no samurai. What do you think, Rikiya? Don't you agree?

NARRATOR: Her ladyship seeks to soften the sharp words.

KAOYO: It does you no good to quarrel. My husband is in trouble now, and I am the cause. The other day, when there was the reception at Tsurugaoka, that monster Moronao made outrageous advances to me, a married woman. He used all his wiles, but I was determined to shame him and teach him a lesson. So, without even telling Lord Hangan, I wrote out the old poem on infidelity, pretending I was asking for his criticism of my own composition, and I sent it to Moronao to put him in his place. But he chose to pay back the disappointment of rejected love by heaping abuse on Lord Hangan. It's not surprising, is it, that my husband, who is short-tempered by nature, was unable to endure this abuse.

NARRATOR: Gōemon and Rikiya can imagine from her description how indignant their master must have been, and their expressions reveal their sympathy.

But the envoy's arrival is announced, and there is a bustle at the entranceway and the reception room. When word reaches the inner apartments her ladyship withdraws from the place of honor, and the three men go to meet the envoys, who come in almost immediately—Ishidō Umanojō and Moronao's close friend, Yakushiji Jirozaemon. As they have come on official business, they walk through the room and without so much as a nod of the head seat themselves in the places of honor. Enya Hangan quietly enters from the next room.

HANGAN: This is indeed an honor. I appreciate your trouble in coming here as the shogun's envoy, Lord Ishidō. (*To servants.*) Bring some saké cups. (*To Ishidō and Yakushiji.*) I should like, when I have heard the contents of the shogun's message, to dispel my gloom by sharing a cup or two with you both.

YAKUSHIJI: An excellent suggestion. I'd like to join you. But I'm afraid that once you've heard His Excellency's command the saké won't get down your throat.

NARRATOR: He laughs contemptuously.

ISHIDŌ: Listen carefully to the order we have brought today as envoys of the shogun.

NARRATOR: He draws out the decree from the breast of his kimono, and unfolds it. Hangan sits in a posture of respectful attention and listens to the words.

ISHIDŌ (*reads*): "Whereas Lord Hangan Takasada, for reasons of a long-standing private quarrel, did attack and wound the chief councilor Kō no Moronao, and disturb the peace in the palace, his lands are confiscated and he is ordered to commit *seppuku.*"

NARRATOR: Kaoyo gasps, and the samurai present exchange glances of consternation. Hangan shows no sign of emotion.

HANGAN: I submit myself in all particulars to His Excellency's command. But now please relax and take a cup of wine, to refresh yourselves after your arduous duties.

YAKUSHIJI: Hold your tongue, Hangan. You should by all rights be strangled and then beheaded for the crime you've committed. You should be grateful that, thanks to His Excellency's clemency, you'll be allowed to commit *seppuku*. I should think you'd start making preparations at once, particularly since there are fixed precedents to be observed when committing *seppuku*. What do you mean by dressing yourself up in a long *haori*,[28] the latest in fashion? Are you drunk? Or are you out of your mind? This is a breach of courtesy towards Lord Ishidō and myself, who've come here by order of the shogun.

NARRATOR: Hangan merely smiles at this harsh rebuke.

HANGAN: I am neither drunk nor out of my mind. As soon as I learned that His Excellency was sending a message today, I knew what to expect. I have prepared myself for my fate, as you can see.

NARRATOR: He lays down his swords and removes his *haori*, revealing death robes—a white, short-sleeved kimono and an unpatterned hempen jacket. All cry out in astonishment. Yakushiji, at a loss for words, pouts in annoyance. Ishidō goes up to Hangan.

ISHIDŌ: I can well imagine what you are going through now. My function is to see to it that the sentence is carried out. Prepare yourself calmly.

HANGAN: I deeply appreciate your kindness. Ever since I wounded him I have been prepared for this. My only regret is that Kakogawa Honzō held me back and kept me from killing Moronao. It rankles in my bones, and I

---

[28] The *haori* is a kind of cloak worn with a kimono. The length of the *haori* was subject to shifts in fashion.

can never forget it. Like Kusunoki Masashige,[29] who declared at Minatogawa that he would prolong his life by the strength of his resolve in his final hours, I vow that I shall be born and die, again and again, until at last I am avenged.

NARRATOR: His voice vibrates with wrath. At the same time a rapping is heard on the sliding door separating this room from the next.

VOICES: We are the retainers of this house. We ask permission to look upon his lordship's face once more, while he is still alive. May we present ourselves before him? Gōemon, please ask on our behalf.

NARRATOR: Gōemon turns to his lordship.

GŌEMON: How shall I answer them, sir?

HANGAN: The request is understandable, but it is quite out of the question before Yuranosuke arrives.

NARRATOR: Gōemon turns to the sliding door.

GŌEMON: You have heard our master's decision. None of you may come in.

NARRATOR: The samurai make no reply, and the room falls silent. Rikiya, acting on his master's orders, takes the dagger which has been readied for this purpose, and places it before him. Hangan calmly slips his hempen jacket from his shoulders and sits more at ease.

HANGAN: The official witnesses are to observe that the sentence has been carried out.

NARRATOR: He draws to him the ceremonial stand and lifts the dagger to his forehead.

HANGAN: Rikiya, Rikiya.

[29] The great hero of the forces loyal to the Emperor Godaigo. Kusunoki died in 1336. The passage in *Taiheiki* alluded to here is in the chapter "The Deaths of Masashige and His Brother."

RIKIYA: Yes, your lordship.

HANGAN: No sign yet of Yuranosuke?

RIKIYA: He hasn't arrived yet, sir.

HANGAN: I am sorry I won't be seeing him again in this life. It's hard to leave him. But there is no helping it. I can wait no longer.

NARRATOR: He takes up the dagger with the point towards him. Plunging it into his left side, he starts to pull it across his abdomen. His wife, too horrified to look, murmurs the invocation to the Buddha, tears in her eyes. The sliding door to the passageway is thrown open and in rushes Ōboshi Yuranosuke. One look at his master and he throws himself down before him in dismay. Senzaki, Yazama, and others of the household rush in after him.

HANGAN: Yuranosuke. I waited for you as long as I could.

YURANOSUKE: To be able to look on your face while you're still alive—

HANGAN: I am pleased, too, very pleased. No doubt you've heard all that has happened. Ah—it's exasperating, humiliating.

YURANOSUKE: I have heard everything. Now that the last moments are upon us, words fail me. All I ask is that you die nobly.

HANGAN: Do you think I need to be reminded?

NARRATOR: With both hands on the dagger, he pulls it across, piercing deep. He gasps with pain.

HANGAN: Yuranosuke, I leave you this dagger as a memento of me. Avenge me!

NARRATOR: He thrusts the point into his windpipe; then, throwing down the bloodstained weapon, he falls forward and breathes his last. His wife and the assembled retainers stand for a moment, transfixed, their eyes shut, their

breaths bated, their teeth clenched; but Yuranosuke crawls
up to his lord and, taking up the dagger, lifts it reverently
to his forehead. He gazes at the bloodstained point and,
clenching his fists, weeps tears of bitter regret. Hangan's
last words have penetrated to his vitals. At this moment
there takes root within Ōboshi that noble purpose which
will give him a name for loyalty and rectitude to resound
through all the ages. Yakushiji suddenly rises to his feet.

YAKUSHIJI (*to retainers.*): Well, now that Hangan has
croaked, you're to turn over the mansion and be quick
about it.

ISHIDŌ: That's no way to talk, Yakushiji. He was the lord of
a province and a castle. Gentlemen, perform the funeral
rites with proper decorum, then quietly leave. My duty
was to serve as the official witness. I have observed the
seppuku and I shall report what I have seen. If you have
anything to ask of me, I will hear it. Please do not hesitate.

NARRATOR: He nods to the assembled retainers and slowly
leaves.

YAKUSHIJI: I'll rest in the back room while they're disposing
of the corpse. Come with me, men.

NARRATOR: He calls to his followers.

YAKUSHIJI: Take whatever rubbish belongs to the retainers
and throw it out the gate. But don't let those newly
fledged *rōnin* swipe any of Hangan's possessions. They're
sure to try hocking them.

NARRATOR: His angry glances dart round the mansion, and
then he goes off to the next room. Her ladyship bursts into
sobs.

KAOYO: Is anything sadder than a samurai's lot in life? I
had so much to tell my husband in his last moments, but
I was ashamed to think the shogun's envoy might despise

me as a sentimental woman, so I kept my grief to myself. How it breaks my heart to look at him!

NARRATOR: She clings to the dead body and weeps, oblivious to everything.

YURANOSUKE: Rikiya, come here. You will go at once with her ladyship and escort the body of our dead master to his family temple, Kōmyōji. I shall overtake you on the way and perform the funeral ceremony. Hori, Yazama, Kodera, Hazama, and the rest of you, guard them.

NARRATOR: At once a palanquin is brought in, borne shoulder high, and set down. The palanquin door is opened, and the retainers approach, weeping all the while, to lay inside the remains of their master. As they silently lift the palanquin her ladyship wails in uncontrollable despair. The retainers comfort her, then all leave with the palanquin, each eager to lead the way, and hurry to the temple. A few, having seen their master's body to the door, return to their seats. Ono Kudayū speaks first.

KUDAYŪ: Master Ōboshi, you succeeded your father, Yawata Rokurō, as chief retainer. I myself am next in line, but from today we are all *rōnin*, with no means of supporting our wives and children. Let us divide among ourselves the public funds of our lord and deliver the mansion at once. Otherwise, we will offend Lord Yakushiji.

YAGORŌ: No, in my opinion, as long as our enemy Kō no Moronao, remains alive, our hatred can only increase. Let us await their attack and make this mansion our final resting place.

SADAKURŌ: What's that? You say we should die here fighting? That's a terrible idea. Our best plan is to do what my father Kudayū proposed—turn over the mansion and divide the money.

NARRATOR: During this discussion Yuranosuke has remained silent, immersed in thought, but at last he speaks.

YURANOSUKE: The opinion Yagorō has expressed is exactly what I myself was thinking. The proper thing to do would be to kill ourselves and follow our late master in death. But rather than simply cutting open our bellies, I have decided it'd be better to await the attack of the Ashikaga troops and die fighting.

KUDAYŪ: Eh? I thought you might have some good counsel for us, but with your typical *rōnin*'s obstinacy, you'd have us trade arrows with Lord Ashikaga. That would be insanity. I'll have nothing to do with it.

SADAKURŌ: Yes, father, you're right. It makes no sense to me either. Let's ask to be left out of this discussion. There's no point in staying here any longer. Let's go.

KUDAYŪ: A good suggestion. Please, gentlemen, don't let us break up your meeting.

NARRATOR: Father and son depart together.

YAGORŌ: Like father, like son, in the money-grubbing Ono family. What cowards to run off, frightened when they heard we'd die fighting! Pay no attention to them, Ōboshi. Go ahead with your plans to meet the attack.

YURANOSUKE: Don't get so excited, Yagorō. What quarrel have we with Lord Ashikaga that we should take arms against him? All I was trying to do when I made that proposal was to sound out the feelings of Kudayū and his son. We will deliver the mansion to Yakushiji and withdraw, each going to his own destination. We will meet again at Yamashina, near the capital, and hold council there, frankly disclosing whatever is in our hearts.

NARRATOR: No sooner has he spoken than Jirozaemon emerges from the next room.

YAKUSHIJI: What a long time it's taking you to make up your minds. If you've disposed of the body, turn over the house at once.

GŌEMON: Yes, I'm sure you've been waiting impatiently. Please examine carefully before you remove them the personal possessions of our late master—his weapons, horse gear, and the rest. Let us leave, Yuranosuke.

YURANOSUKE: Very well.

NARRATOR: They silently get to their feet. At the thought that today they look for the last time on this mansion where, for generations of their master's ancestors, their own ancestors served day and night, they feel such reluctance to leave that they turn back again and again. When at last they step out the gate, Rikiya, Yazama, Hori, and Kodera, who have escorted the funeral procession, return running.

RIKIYA: Have you turned over the mansion? Now we have only to wait for Tadayoshi's troops. We'll die fighting.

NARRATOR: His voice is excited, but Yuranosuke calms him.

YURANOSUKE: No, this is not the time for us to die. Look at this, all of you.

NARRATOR: He unsheathes the memento left by their late master.

YURANOSUKE: This dagger, its tip stained with our master's blood, preserves his soul still, and it cries out for vengeance. With this dagger we will cut off Moronao's head and accomplish our mission.

NARRATOR: The others enthusiastically assent. Inside the mansion Yakushiji Jirō orders the bar of the great gate thrust into place.

YAKUSHIJI: The crime against Lord Moronao has been punished. It serves them right.

NARRATOR: His followers clap their hands with joy, and their voices roaring with laughter rise into a war cry.

SAMURAI: Listen to that!

NARRATOR: A young samurai turns back, but Yuranosuke cries out.

YURANOSUKE: Have you no wish to avenge our master?

NARRATOR: They shout in agreement and start out together, but turn back again and again to glare with resentment at the mansion, before at last they leave.

Act Five

NARRATOR: A hawk may be starving, but he will not pick up fallen grains of rice, the saying goes. Here, in a lonely dwelling near Yamazaki,[30] where the moon sinks into the mountains, Hayano Kampei has spent many days, condemned by the fault of his youthful spirits to eke out a scant existence, following trails through the mountains in pursuit of deer and monkeys. Hunting is his livelihood, and he carries a gun in readiness, but his sleeves are soaked by a bulletlike rain that comes shooting down. Who was it called this the "Rainless Month"?[31] As he takes shelter under a pine, waiting for a letup in the evening shower, a traveler, a samurai like himself, comes hurrying along the dark road from the opposite direction, braving the heavy rain and shielding with the skirts of his cloak, to keep the rain from extinguishing it, a little lantern braced with arched bamboo.

KAMPEI: Excuse me. I'm sorry to startle you, but could you kindly give me a light?

[30] A town between Kyoto and Osaka.

[31] "Rainless month" was a poetic name for the sixth month, actually a time of monsoonlike rain.

77

NARRATOR: He goes up to the traveler, who is at once on guard.

TRAVELER: Hmmm. I travel alone on this road, but I know how dangerous it is. I see you're a hunter and you carry a gun. I'm not giving you a light. Ask someone else.

NARRATOR: He throws Kampei a look that seems to say one move and he will strike.

KAMPEI: I understand. It's natural you should mistake me for a bandit. I hunt in this neighborhood, but the heavy rain has soaked my match-rope, and now I don't know what to do. Here, I'll let you hold my gun, and borrow the light myself.

NARRATOR: These straightforward words make the man stare into Kampei's face.

TRAVELER: Am I mistaken in thinking you are Hayano Kampei?

KAMPEI: And you're Senzaki Yagorō!

YAGORŌ: I'm glad you are all right.

KAMPEI: It's good to see you again.

NARRATOR: At this first meeting after long separation bitter, unforgettable resentment over the fall of their master's house wells up in their hearts, and both men clench their fists. Kampei bows his head, and for a time remains speechless.

KAMPEI: I'm so ashamed of my disgrace I can't lift my head even before an old friend like yourself. I wonder if my luck as a samurai has completely run out? It was my unavoidable misfortune that the disaster to our house occurred when I was waiting on Lord Hangan. I couldn't go back to the mansion, not having been with our master when he needed me. I decided that my best plan would be to wait for some occasion when I might beg his forgiveness. I never expected he would commit *seppuku*. When I heard the news I thought, "This is all Moronao's dirty work!" I put my hand on my sword, thinking that at least I could escort our master on the road to death. But then I asked myself what I had ever done to merit escorting him. I racked my brains to think how I could dare show myself or excuse my behavior. Just then I got wind of rumors that Yuranosuke, his son Rikiya, Gōemon, and the others had been meeting with the intention of planning revenge for our master. Whatever my faults, I was never actually disowned by our master. If I could find some way of meeting Yuranosuke and persuading him to let me add my seal to those of the others in the league, my honor would be restored through this and all lives to come. What a miraculous piece of good luck it has been to meet you! [32] Please, I beg you, give me the chance to restore my honor as a samurai. For the sake of our old friendship as retainers of the same master, for the sake of your fellow feelings as a samurai, I implore you.

NARRATOR: He touches his hands to the ground and weeps a man's tears of remorse over his past mistake, tears that are the more pitiful for being so understandable. Yagorō, though he sympathizes with his comrade, is not free to divulge the great plan.

YAGORŌ: Kampei, what nonsense is this—mixing talk of a plot and a league and heaven knows what else with excuses for your misbehavior? There's nothing in the rumors. I am on my way with an urgent message from Yuranosuke

[32] Literally, "to make the flowers of the *udonge* bloom." The *udonge* was a flower, mentioned in Indian legends, that bloomed only once in 3,000 years; for Kampei to come across Yagorō by accident has been as lucky as happening to be present on the rare occasion of the blooming of the *udonge*.

to Gōemon. We plan to erect a monument to our late master at his grave. Being mere *rōnin*, we must collect money in order to erect a worthy memorial, for we know people in ages to come will point it out as Lord Enya Hangan's monument. That is my errand now. We are anxious to select only men who are still grateful for our late master's kindness. That is why I cannot speak out more plainly about this great undertaking. If you still feel grateful to our master . . . Do you follow me, Kampei?

NARRATOR: Truly it was the friendship of old comrades that made him reveal indirectly Ōboshi's scheme, under the guise of discussing a monument.

KAMPEI: I'm most grateful to you, Yagorō. Yes, I had heard some time ago you were raising funds for a monument, and I have done what I could to put together some money, hoping I might be pardoned on the strength of my contribution. But no matter how I rack my brains, Yagorō, I am, to my shame, reduced to these circumstances—the punishment our master has imposed on me. There is no one I can turn to for financial help. But Okaru's father Yoichibei is a reliable man. He is only a farmer, but he bitterly regrets that Okaru and I were disloyal to Lord Hangan. He and my mother-in-law have begged me in tears to find some means of becoming a samurai again. When I tell them of my good fortune in meeting you, and the details of our conversation, and inform them that I intend to become a samurai again, I am sure Yoichibei won't refuse, for his children's sake, to sell the little land he owns. Please pass this on to Gōemon, when you give him the money for the fund. I beg you.

NARRATOR: His tone is desperate.

YAGORŌ: I see. Very well, I'll tell Gōemon your story, and ask him to plead for you with Yuranosuke. I promise definitely to give you an answer by the day after tomorrow. Here is the address where Gōemon is staying.

NARRATOR: He hands a paper to Kampei, who lifts it reverently.

KAMPEI: I am grateful for all your many kindnesses. I will manage somehow to raise the money as soon as possible, and I expect to have the honor of seeing you the day after tomorrow. If you wish to visit my house, turn left at the Yamazaki ferry crossing and ask for Yoichibei's. You'll find it without any trouble. But you'd best be on your way before it gets dark. The road is even more dangerous farther on. Be on your guard.

YAGORŌ: Don't worry. Not even a flea's going to bite me until the monument is raised. You, too, take care of yourself. I'll be waiting for word of your contribution. Good-by until then.

NARRATOR: They separate, each hurrying on his way. Again the rain comes pounding down, and there is a sound of tottering footsteps, an old man trudging his way along the path, stick in hand, not lost because of the darkness, but in the dark because of love of his child; [33] an honest old man, upright as the staff he carries. From behind him on the path a voice calls.

SADAKURŌ: Hey there! Hey you, old man! Wait up! I'll go with you.

NARRATOR: This is Sadakurō, Ono Kudayū's son. Knowing no other way to make a living, he has become a highwayman,

---

[33] A poem by Fujiwara Kanesuke in *Gosen Shū*: "Even though a parent's heart may not be in darkness, it will wander on the path of love for his child."

and nightly plies his trade along this road. He wears a broad sword slung downwards around his waist.

SADAKURŌ: I've been calling you for the longest time. Didn't you hear me? You're certainly brave, at your age, to travel along this dangerous road. I thought I'd join you.

NARRATOR: He circles round and stares curiously at the old man, who shudders with fright, but shows the cunning of the aged.

OLD MAN: One doesn't expect such kindness from a young man. I'm getting on in years, and I don't like traveling alone, but no matter where you go, nothing is so important as money. I couldn't pay my taxes last year and I've just been to visit some relatives to ask their help, but I didn't raise a penny. I couldn't very well overstay my welcome where I wasn't making any headway, so I left for home alone, completely discouraged.

NARRATOR: Sadakurō interrupts.

SADAKURŌ: Cut the chatter. I'm not here to give advice about your arrears on last year's taxes. Look here, old man. Listen carefully to what I say. This is the situation. I noticed a while back that you were carrying a striped wallet. It must hold forty to fifty ryō if the contents are gold, and that's why I've followed you. I'd like you to lend me that money. I'm pleading with you as a man, on bended knee. I suppose you've got the money because you're in trouble of some sort, or maybe it's your kid, the sort of thing that happens all the time. But I've set my eyes on your wallet, and there's nothing you can do about it. Make up your mind to that. Lend it to me, please.

NARRATOR: He thrusts his hand into the old man's bosom and pulls out the striped wallet.

OLD MAN: Excuse me, but that's only—

SADAKURŌ: What do you mean "that's only" when you've got all this money?

NARRATOR: The old man clutches at Sadakurō's hand as he snatches away the wallet.

OLD MAN: It's true, I took some small coins from this wallet to buy straw sandals at the last village, but all that's left in it now are some rice balls for my lunch and the medicines my daughter gave me for my dizziness. Please let me go, sir.

NARRATOR: He snatches back the wallet and tries to run away, but Sadakurō intercepts him.

SADAKURŌ: You obstinate fool! I spoke to you gently because I didn't want to hurt you, only to have you take advantage of me! Fork over the money! I'll finish you off with one blow if you're slow about it.

NARRATOR: He lifts his sword in both hands, and before the old man can even cry out, Sadakurō slashes downwards, as if splitting a stalk of bamboo. The blow misses the mark—a fault of the sword or of the hand? The old man clutches the naked blade in his hands.

OLD MAN: You've made up your mind to kill me, then?

SADAKURŌ: Of course I have. That's what I do when I see somebody with money. Stop your complaining and croak!

NARRATOR: He points the blade at the old man's chest.

OLD MAN: Wait, please wait, sir. I see there's no helping it. It's true this wallet contains money, but the money is the price of my only daughter. This daughter has a husband who's more precious to her than life itself. Her husband needs this money. He became a *rōnin* because of a little trouble he had, and my daughter insists it was her fault. She keeps pleading every night with my wife and me to do something so he can become a samurai again. But we're

poor people. We have no way to raise the money. I've
discussed the matter with my wife from every angle. Finally we hit on a plan that we got our daughter to accept,
and we agreed to keep it absolutely secret from my son-in-
law. This money is the tears of blood the three of us have
shed. If you take it away, what will become of my daughter? See, I bow before you. Please spare my life. You look
as if you were once a samurai yourself. Samurai should
show compassion for one another. Without this money
my daughter and my son will never be able to hold up
their heads in the world. He is the husband of my only
child and I feel pity and love for him. I beg you, forgive
me and spare my life. You're still young and you probably
haven't any children yet, but one day you'll have a child
and you'll know what I have said is the truth. So please
let me leave safely. My house is just a couple of miles
away. As soon as I've turned over the money to my son-in-
law you can kill me if you like. I beg you. Let me see the
joy on my daughter's face before I die. Please listen.

NARRATOR: He begs for mercy, but his voice trails off into
distant echoes that only increase the pathos.

SADAKURŌ: Well, if that isn't just too sad! Go on, howl your
fill, you old wreck. If this money brings me success your
act of charity should bring your son success too. A good
deed done another is never rewarded with evil, they say.
It's too bad for you!

NARRATOR: He thrusts his sword in deep and the old man's
limbs flail in agony. Sadakurō kicks him around as he
writhes.

SADAKURŌ: Oh, what a pitiful sight! I'm sure it must hurt,
but don't hold any grudges against me. I've killed you
because of the money you had. Why should I ever have

harmed you if you hadn't had any money? Your money was your enemy, not I, you poor old man. *Namu Amida. Namu Myōhō Rengekyō.* Go to heaven, whichever one you prefer.[34]

NARRATOR: He does not even pull out the sword, but thrusts it deeper and twists it in the wound. The bushes and leaves are dewed with crimson as the old man wretchedly breathes his last, in extreme agony. Satisfied with his accomplishment, Sadakurō picks up the wallet and in the darkness calculates the contents by touch.

SADAKURŌ: Fifty *ryō!* It's a long time since I've had the pleasure of your company! Thanks for the visit!

NARRATOR: Slinging the wallet round his neck, he pushes and kicks the corpse into the valley below. Unaware that mud from the corpse has spattered his own body, he stands there a moment, when he sees behind him a wounded boar charging headlong in his direction. He leaps aside in alarm. The wild boar rushes on unswervingly, snorting, kicking up roots and stones, and scattering clumps of mud and twigs. Sadakurō watches as it dashes by him, only for two shots to rip through his body, from his spine to his ribs. Not uttering so much as a groan or cry, he tumbles over backwards and dies, a heartwarming sight. Kampei, supposing he has killed the boar, gropes here and there, gun in hand, but when he finds and raises his prey, it is no wild boar.

KAMPEI: Good heavens! I've killed a man. What a disaster!

NARRATOR: In the utter darkness he cannot tell who has been shot. He lifts the man in his arms, thinking he might

---

[34] *Namu Amida (Butsu)* is the invocation of believers in Pure Land Buddhism; *Namu Myōhō Rengekyō* is used by believers in Nichiren Buddhism. Sadakurō is offering Yoichibei his choice of paradise.

still be breathing, when his hands touch the wallet of
gold. Kampei can tell from the feel that it contains forty
or fifty *ryō*. He lifts it reverently to his forehead, sure it is
a gift from heaven, and rushes off, all but flying, even
swifter than the boar.

Act Six

NARRATOR:

> The dance at Misaki is just at its height,
> Grandpa, won't you go?
> Take old grandma, take her along,
> Grandpa, won't you go?

This is the song the farmers sing when pounding barley, here at Yamazaki, famed in story, where Yoichibei, a small farmer, has his humble cottage. Here too Hayano Kampei lives the secluded life of a *rōnin*. His wife Okaru opens her comb box, to tidy her hair disheveled by sleep. Dawn is near, but still her husband does not return. To pass the tedious hours waiting for him, she combs and binds her locks into a hanging bun. As she passes the wet comb of boxwood through her hair her mind fills with thoughts of the unspeakable fate she can reveal to no one. She combs a lovely sheen into her tresses, and when she ties them elegantly such beauty seems wasted in a country place. Her aged mother comes tottering home, learning on a stick, along the path through the fields.

MOTHER: Oh, you've done up your hair, daughter! You've

arranged it very nicely. Everywhere you go in the country at this time of year people are busy harvesting barley. Just now as I passed the bamboo grove I heard the young men singing the barley-pounders' song—"Grandpa, won't you go? Take old grandma, take her along." That reminded me how late the old man is in coming home. I was so worried I went all the way to the end of the village, but it didn't do any good. There wasn't a sign of him.

OKARU: Yes, I wonder why he's so late. I'll run out and have a look.

MOTHER: No, a young woman should never go outside alone. Why, you never liked walking around the village even when you were a little girl. That's why we sent you into service with Lord Enya. But something must have drawn you back to this out-of-the-way place. I've never even seen you look bored as long as Kampei was with you.

OKARU: That's natural, Mother. It doesn't bother me to live in poverty, let alone in a village, when I'm with the man I love. The Bon Festival will be here soon, and Kampei and I plan to go see the dancing, just the two of us, the way it goes in the song, "Papa, won't you go? Take mama, take her along." I'm sure you remember what it was like when you were young.

NARRATOR: The forthright girl speaks her mind freely, and her spirits seem buoyant.

MOTHER: You sound cheerful, full of fun, but in your heart, I know—

OKARU: No, Mother. I'm resigned to it. I've long since made up my mind to go into service at Gion, for my husband's sake. But for Father, at his age, to take all this trouble—

MOTHER: You shouldn't say that. Your brother, after all, was a retainer of Lord Enya, though he had only a minor position, so it isn't like taking trouble for a stranger.

NARRATOR: As they are talking, along the road, urging his palanquin ahead, comes Ichimonjiya from Gion.

ICHIMONJIYA: This is the place.

NARRATOR: He calls from the gate as he goes in.

ICHIMONJIYA: Is Master Yoichibei at home?

MOTHER: Oh, what a surprise! You've certainly come a long distance! Daughter, bring out the tobacco and offer our guest some tea.

NARRATOR: Mother and daughter, in a flurry of excitement, wait on him. The master of the brothel speaks.

ICHIMONJIYA: It was extremely kind of the old gentleman to have visited my place last night. I trust he returned home safely?

MOTHER: You mean you haven't brought him back with you? This is strange. Ever since he set out for your place—

ICHIMONJIYA: He hasn't come back? How peculiar. I wonder if he strolled past the Inari Shrine and was bewitched by a fox? At any rate, we agreed without difficulty, as we had decided when I came here the other day, that your daughter's term of service will be a full five years, and that her wages will be one hundred *ryō* in gold. The old gentleman told me he had to deliver the money tonight, and begged me in tears to let him sign the bond of service last evening so that he might receive the hundred *ryō* in advance. I agreed to pay him half the sum on signing the bond and the balance on receipt of the girl. In any case, he was overjoyed when I gave him the fifty *ryō*, and he lifted the money to his forehead. He was still babbling on when he left, it must have been about ten o'clock. I tried to stop him, saying it was dangerous to walk alone on the road at night when one is carrying money, but he wouldn't listen to me. He left for home, but I wonder if on the way—

OKARU: No, there was nowhere for him to stop was there, Mother?

MOTHER: No, of course not. By all rights he should've come rushing back, all out of breath, eager to get home the first possible moment so he could make us happy by showing us the money. I can't understand it.

ICHIMONJIYA: Well, whether you can understand it or not, that's your problem. I intend to deliver the balance of the money and take my new employee with me.

NARRATOR: He produces the money.

ICHIMONJIYA: Here are the remaining fifty *ryō*. This makes a total of one hundred *ryō*. Please take them.

MOTHER: But, Okaru, I can't let you go, can I, before your father gets back.

ICHIMONJIYA: If you keep dawdling we'll never be finished. Look, this is Yoichibei's seal, there's no disputing it. The bond of service is my witness. I have this day with my money bought the girl's body. One day's delay in delivery means so much loss for me. It looks as if I have no choice but to do it this way.

NARRATOR: He seizes the girl's hand and drags her to her feet.

MOTHER: Wait, I beg you!

NARRATOR: He shakes off the mother's clutching hand, and with brute force pushes Okaru into his palanquin. As the bearers lift the shafts, Kampei appears at the gate, gun in hand, wearing his straw raincoat and hat. He strides boldly in.

KAMPEI: Where are they taking my wife?

MOTHER: You've come back in the nick of time, Kampei.

NARRATOR: He does not understand his mother's joy.

KAMPEI: There's something at the bottom of this. Mother, Okaru, I'd like to know what's going on.

NARRATOR: He seats himself squarely in the middle of the room. The master of the Ichimonjiya speaks.

ICHIMONJIYA: I take it you are my employee's husband. But there's nothing you can do about this. I have it in the bond, signed and sealed by the old man, that "no contravention or interference in the execution of this contract will be permitted, even by the husband or fiancé of the employee." I intent to collect my employee now.

MOTHER: You must be wondering what all this means, Kampei. We've heard for a long time from Okaru about how badly you needed money, and we spoke of nothing but of how much we wanted to raise it for you, but we had nowhere to turn for even a copper coin. Then your father suggested that perhaps you had thought of selling your wife to raise the money. Of course, this was most unlikely, but it might be that you felt constrained because of your wife's parents. Your father said, "The best thing would be for me to sell my daughter without telling Kampei. When a samurai is desperate he'll even turn to crime, they say. It's no disgrace to sell his wife—the money is for his lord's sake. If we raise the money and give it to him, I'm sure he won't be angry with us." So yesterday he went to Gion to settle the matter, but he hasn't come home yet. Okaru and I were worrying about him when the gentleman came and said he gave Father half the money last night and was going to pay us the balance now and take Okaru with him. I begged him to wait until we had seen Father, but he wouldn't listen. He was just about to take Okaru away. What shall we do, Kampei?

KAMPEI: To begin with, I must tell you how grateful I am for Father's solicitude. But I have had rather a piece of luck myself, which I'll tell you about in a moment, and

I'm not turning over my wife until my father gets back.

ICHIMONJIYA: Why not?

KAMPEI: Well, he's her father and the man who signed the
bond. You claim you paid him half the money, fifty ryō in
gold, last night. No doubt that's true, but—

ICHIMONJIYA: Do you realize who I am? I'm Ichimonjiya. I
cover the whole Kyoto-Osaka area, and I've enough women
in my employ to populate the Island of Dames.[35] Would
I say I'd paid him the money if I hadn't? But I have even
more positive proof. When I saw your old man wrap up
the fifty ryō in his little towel and tuck it into his kimono,
I said, "That's dangerous. Put it in this and carry it around
your neck." I lent him a wallet made out of striped cloth,
the same material as this kimono I'm wearing. He's sure
to be coming back soon with the wallet round his neck.

KAMPEI: What did you say? Did you say the wallet was
made from the same striped material as your kimono?

ICHIMONJIYA: That's right.

KAMPEI: The exact same striped material?

ICHIMONJIYA: What more positive proof could there be?

NARRATOR: Kampei is stunned. He glances cautiously around
him, then takes the wallet from his sleeve and compares
it with the kimono. Both are of a mixed cotton and silk
striped cloth, absolutely identical in pattern.

KAMPEI: Good heavens! Was the man I shot last night my
father-in-law?

NARRATOR: A pain shoots through him more severe than if
the two bullets had pierced his own breast. His wife, knowing nothing of his anguish, asks.

OKARU: Kampei, please don't hesitate so, but make up your
mind whether you're going to send me away or not.

---

[35] Nyogo no shima, a mythical island populated entirely by women.

KAMPEI: Oh, yes. He's given such convincing proof I don't suppose we have any choice but to let you go, have we?

OKARU: Without seeing Father?

KAMPEI: I ran into your father briefly this morning. There's no telling when he'll get back.

OKARU: Then you saw Father? Why didn't you say so, instead of making Mother and me worry?

NARRATOR: Ichimonjiya takes advantage of the situation.

ICHIMONJIYA: Ask seven times before you suspect a man, they say. Now that we know where the old man is, it's a big load off your minds and mine too. If you still have any complaints to make, whatever they may be, we'll leave them for a court to decide. Anyway, I'm glad everything has been settled. I hope the old folks will pay me a little visit when you worship at Rokujō.[36] Come now, into the palanquin with you.

OKARU: Yes, yes. Kampei—I'm going now. From now on it's up to you to look after my old parents, especially Father—he's got a bad complaint. Please take good care of him.

NARRATOR: Not having the slightest suspicion her father is dead, she makes this request, so pathetic, so touching that Kampei wonders if he shouldn't confess and tell her the whole truth. But others are present; so he bears in silence the agony in his heart.

MOTHER: I'm sure Kampei would like to take a proper leave of you and say good-by like a husband to his wife. He must be afraid you'll break down.

OKARU: There's no danger of that. I'm leaving my husband, it's true, but I'm selling myself for our master's sake, so I

36 A reference to Nishi Hongan-ji, a great temple of Shin Buddhism situated in Rokujō, Kyoto.

don't feel sad or anything like that. I go in good spirits, Mother. I am only sorry I'm leaving without seeing Father.

MOTHER: I'm sure he'll go and visit you as soon as he gets back.

OKARU: Take moxa treatment so you don't get sick, and please come see me, so I'll know you're all right.

MOTHER: Oh, if you haven't handkerchiefs or a fan you'll need them. Have you everything else? Don't rush about too much and hurt yourself.

NARRATOR: She fusses over Okaru until the girl is actually inside the palanquin. As they bid each other good-by, she wonders what ill fate has decreed that a daughter as attractive as the next girl should have to experience such sadness. She clenches her teeth and weeps, and her daughter, clinging to the sides of the palanquin, stifles her sobs, afraid lest her tears be seen or heard. The bearers, indifferent to their grief, lift the chair and hurry down the road. The mother gazes after them.

MOTHER: I'm sure I upset Okaru by saying such foolish things. Kampei, I hope you won't keep fretting over your wife. You'll only make yourself sick. I'm her mother, but you saw how bravely I've resigned myself. I wonder why Father hasn't returned. You said you saw him, didn't you?

KAMPEI: That's right.

MOTHER: Where was it you met him? And where did he go after he left you?

KAMPEI: Let me see. The place where I left him was Toba, I think. Or was it Fushimi or Yodo or perhaps Takeda?

NARRATOR: As he speaks this nonsense—whatever comes to his lips—Big-Mouth Yahachi, Roku the Musketeer, and Kakuhei the Badger, three hunters of the vicinity, burst unceremoniously into the room. They bear the body of the old man, covered with a straw raincoat, on a shutter.

YAHACHI: I was going home after finishing my hunting for the night when I stumbled across your old man. He's been killed. Me and these other hunters brought him back.

NARRATOR: The mother starts in amazement at his words.

MOTHER: Who did it, Kampei—what monster could have killed him? You must kill the murderer! Oh, my husband, my dear husband!

NARRATOR: She calls and shrieks, but in vain; for her there are only tears. The huntsmen speak one after the other.

HUNTER A: Poor old lady! It must be sad for you.

HUNTER B: You should report this to the district office and get them to investigate.

HUNTER C: It's a terrible shame.

NARRATOR: They go out together, each bound for his own home. The mother, still weeping, moves closer to Kampei.

MOTHER: I've fought against the thought you might possibly, conceivably have anything to do with this, Kampei. But there is one thing I don't understand. I know you used to be a samurai, but still, you should have acted a little more surprised when you saw your father-in-law's dead body. Are you sure you didn't receive the money when you met him on the road? What did he say to you? Tell me, please. What does this mean? You don't seem to have an answer, do you? And here's the reason why!

NARRATOR: She thrusts her hand into Kampei's kimono and pulls out the wallet.

MOTHER: I caught a glimpse of this wallet a while ago. Look —it's stained with blood. You killed your father.

KAMPEI: No, you see—

MOTHER: What do you mean "you see"? No matter how
hard you try to hide the truth, it won't stay hidden.
Heaven will reveal it. You killed your father and robbed
him. And for whose sake do you suppose that money was
intended? I know what happened. You thought your
father, because he was poor, had intercepted half the
money he got from selling his daughter, and that he would
pocket half of it and not give you the whole amount. So
you killed him and took the money for yourself. It makes
my blood boil that I was always deceived into supposing,
until this very moment, that you were a decent, upright
man. You monster! You revolt me so I can't even cry.
Poor Yoichibei. You never realized what a beast you had
for a son-in-law. You were so anxious for him to become
a samurai again, the way he used to be, that you went
running all over Kyoto, a man of your age, not resting
even at night, throwing away your own money—and everything you did to help him has harmed yourself. Your
hand has been bitten by the dog you fed. Who could
have imagined you would be killed in such a horrible way?

And as for you, you fiend, you serpent! Give me back
my husband! Give him back to me alive!

NARRATOR: All restraint and politeness lost, she seizes the
man by his topknot and, pulling him down, beats his head
against the floor.

MOTHER: I could hack you to pieces and still my anger
would not be appeased.

NARRATOR: She falls prostrate on the floor, still muttering
her resentment. Boiling hot sweat pours over Kampei's
whole body for the crime he has committed. He presses
his face into the matting. Now he knows what it is to
suffer the wrath of heaven.

Two samurai, their faces covered by wicker hats, appear at the door.

GŌEMON: Is Hayano Kampei at home? Hara Gōemon and Senzaki Yagorō would like to see him.

NARRATOR: Their visit comes at the worst possible moment, but Kampei goes to meet them, his rudely made sword under his arm.

KAMPEI: I am deeply grateful, gentlemen, that you should have condescended to visit such a humble cottage.

NARRATOR: He bows his head.

GŌEMON: There seems to have been some misfortune in this house.

KAMPEI: A minor domestic matter. Please pay no attention to it, but come right in.

GŌEMON: Then, with your permission, we shall do so.

NARRATOR: They go straight in and seat themselves. Kampei bows, both hands on the floor.

KAMPEI: I was gravely at fault not to have been present when the terrible misfortune befell our master. I have not a word to say in my defense. But I implore you, gentlemen, to intercede on my behalf so that my offense may be pardoned and I may be permitted to attend with the others of the clan the services on the anniversary of our master's death.

NARRATOR: He speaks in terms of humble supplication. Gōemon at once responds.

GŌEMON: Yuranosuke was at first most impressed that you, a *rōnin* of no means, should have offered such a large sum as your contribution for the monument. But then he said, "We are erecting this monument so that we may promote the salvation of our late master. It would not please his spirit if we paid for the monument with money taken from

a man who had proved disloyal and faithless to his lordship." The money is therefore being returned, the seal
still unbroken.

NARRATOR: Yagorō takes the money from his kimono and
lays it before Kampei, who is speechless with bewilderment. The mother, still weeping, speaks.

MOTHER (to Kampei): You loathsome villain! Do you
know now what a father's vengeance is? (To Gōemon
and Yagorō.) Gentlemen, please listen to me. My husband, old though he was, gave no thought to his own
future happiness, but sold his daughter for his son-in-law's
sake. He was returning with the money he had raised
when this monster ambushed him. This is the money he
took after killing his father. How can such money be of
use to you, as long as there is a God in heaven? I'll never
believe in the gods or buddhas again if this patricide and
vile robber is not punished. Strike this unfilial beast and
kill him by inches! Ah—I'm seething with rage!

NARRATOR: She throws herself down on the floor and weeps.
The two men, astonished by her words, draw their swords
and close in on Kampei from either side. Yagorō's voice
is harsh.

YAGORŌ: Kampei, I never suggested you atone for your
offense by taking money in such an inhuman, unspeakable way. It would be useless trying to explain to you
what it means to be a samurai. You're a double criminal.
You've killed your father-in-law—that's the same as a
father—and robbed him of his money. You should be
skewered on a spear like a string of dumplings, and I intend to do precisely that!

NARRATOR: He glares at Kampei.

GŌEMON: The just man takes it as his maxim that no matter

how thirsty he may be he will not drink water from a spring thieves have drunk from. Did you suppose that the money you took after killing your father-in-law could be spent in our master's cause? I marvel all the more at Yuranosuke's acumen in spurning your money. He intuitively recognized that the man who offered it was corrupt and disloyal through and through. The unfortunate thing is that word of this will get around, and people may say that Hayano Kampei, a retainer of Enya Hangan, committed a monstrous crime. This will disgrace not only you but our late master. Didn't you realize that? You blockhead— you never used to be so stupid you couldn't understand something so obvious. What devil has got into you?

NARRATOR: Tears blur his sharp eyes. Kampei, unable to withstand these arguments and dogged questions, slips his kimono from his shoulders, draws his dagger, and instantly plunges the blade into his abdomen.

KAMPEI: I am ashamed to appear before you in these humiliating circumstances. I had made up my mind to commit *seppuku* if you refused my request. I'll tell you everything since, as you say, the crime of killing my father reflects disgrace on our late master. Please hear me out. Last evening, on my way home after leaving Yagorō, I sighted a wild boar running over the hill in the dusk. I stopped it with two shots. I ran up and searched for it, only to find I had shot not a wild boar but a man. I was dumfounded at my terrible mistake. I felt in his bosom for some medicine, but I discovered instead a wallet containing this money. It was wrong of me, I know, but it seemed like money from heaven, so I rushed off to Yagorō and gave it to him. When I got back home I learned what had happened. The man I killed was my father-in-law and the money the price of my wife. Everything I do goes at cross purposes, like the crossbill's beak. My luck as a samurai seems to have run out. Try to imagine how this fate afflicts me!

NARRATOR: Tears of chagrin are in his bloodshot eyes. Yagorō rises as soon as he has heard this account. He lifts the dead body, turns it over, and examines the wounds.

YAGORŌ: Gōemon, will you come here? These look like gunshot wounds, but they've been gouged out with a sword. Kampei, you acted too quickly!

NARRATOR: The wounded man looks up in surprise, and his mother is amazed. Gōemon has a sudden recollection.

GŌEMON: It makes sense now, Senzaki. You remember that on our way here we saw the dead body of a traveler. When we examined it, we found the man had been killed by a bullet. It was Ono Sadakurō, a ruffian so depraved even his rapacious old father Kudayū had disowned him and refused ever to see him again. I remember hearing that Sadakurō had become a highwayman for want of any other occupation. Undoubtedly it was he who murdered Kampei's father-in-law.

MOTHER: You mean, it wasn't Kampei who killed my husband?

NARRATOR: She clings to the wounded man with a shriek of dismay.

MOTHER: Kampei, I bow before you. I entreat you. I made a terrible mistake in abusing you. It was all an old woman's foolishness. Forgive me, please, Kampei, and don't die, don't die.

NARRATOR: She weeps, pleading with him. He lifts his head.

KAMPEI: This moment, when my mother's suspicions have been allayed and the blot on my honor removed, will be the remembrance I take with me to the afterworld. I shall catch up with my father-in-law and accompany him to the Mountain of Death and the River of Three Ways.

NARRATOR: He starts to pull the dagger across his belly.

GŌEMON: Wait, wait! You killed your father-in-law's enemy without even intending to. Doesn't that show your luck as a samurai still holds? Kampei, you have, by the mercy of the god of war, performed a deed of great merit. I have something secret to show you while you still breathe.

NARRATOR: He takes out a scroll and quickly unrolls it.

GŌEMON: Here are the signatures of the men in our league. We have exchanged written oaths to the gods that we will kill Kō no Moronao, our master's enemy.

NARRATOR: Kampei, in agony, cannot read through the whole.

KAMPEI: Whose names are there?

GŌEMON: There are forty-five in all. Now that we have seen your true character, we will add you to our league and make our number forty-six. Take this remembrance with you to the afterworld.

NARRATOR: He takes out a writing kit and inscribes Kampei's name.

GŌEMON: Seal it with your blood, Kampei.

KAMPEI: I will.

NARRATOR: He cuts his belly in a cross and, pulling out his entrails, presses them to the paper.

KAMPEI: I have sealed the document in my blood. Ahhh, how grateful, how thankful I am! My long-cherished wish has become a reality. Mother, please do not grieve. Father's death and my wife's becoming a prostitute have not been in vain. Offer this money as our contribution to the league.

NARRATOR: His mother, still weeping, places before the two men the wallet and the packets of money.

MOTHER: Kampei's soul is in this wallet. Think of it as being my son and take it with you when you go to kill our enemy.

GŌEMON: We will. That would be most appropriate.

NARRATOR: Gōemon takes the money.

GŌEMON: It occurs to me now that the gold in the striped wallet stands for the rays of purplish gold emanating from the Buddha. May your worthy deeds obtain your Buddha's happiness!

KAMPEI: Buddha's happiness! I spurn it! I refuse to die, I refuse. My soul shall stay on earth and go with you when you attack.

NARRATOR: His voice trembles with agony. His mother is blinded by tears.

MOTHER: Kampei, I wish I could let my daughter know this, so she could at least see you before you die.

KAMPEI: No, mother. Tell her, if you wish, of her father's death, but please never reveal that I am dead. My wife was sold for our master's sake, but if she learns of my death and then neglects her service, it would be just the same as if she were disloyal to our master. Leave things as they are. I die content.

NARRATOR: He drives the point of his dagger into his throat and falls forward, breathing his last.

MOTHER: Kampei, are you dead so soon? Is there in all the world another person as unlucky as myself? My husband is dead, and the son-in-law who was my support has gone before me. My beloved daughter is still alive, but we have been torn apart. How can I, an old woman left alone in the world, go on living? Dear husband, Yoichibei, please take me with you.

NARRATOR: She flings herself on the body, weeping and wailing, then stands again.

MOTHER: Kampei, your mother is going with you.

NARRATOR: She clings to him and sinks to the floor. She weeps first over one of the dead, then over the other, until at last she collapses with a shriek, sobbing unrestrainedly, a sight too pitiful to behold. Gōemon rises.

GŌEMON: You have every cause to weep, old lady. I am sure Ōboshi will be gratified when I report how Kampei died and give him Kampei's contribution. This money that was slung round his neck is fifty *ryō* for the forty-nine days of prayer for your husband and son-in-law, a hundred *ryō* in all for a hundred days of mourning. Pray for them devoutly. And now farewell. Farewell.

NARRATOR: Tears are in her eyes as she watches them depart, and tears blur their eyes too as they look back, waves of tears that rise between them in this world of sadness.

Act Seven

NARRATOR: If you would dally among flowers you will find in Gion a full range of colors. East, south, north, and west, with a glitter as bright as if Amida's Pure Land has been gilded anew, Gion sparkles with courtesans and geishas, so lovely as to steal away the senses of even the most jaded man, and leave him a raving fool.

KUDAYŪ: Is anybody here? Where's the master? Master!

MASTER: Rush, rush, rush! Who's there? Whom have I the pleasure of serving? Why, it's Master Ono Kudayū! How formal of you to ask to be shown in!

KUDAYŪ: I've brought a gentleman with me who's here for the first time. You seem awfully busy, but have you a room you can show this gentleman?

MASTER: Indeed I have, sir. Tonight that big spender Yuranosuke had the bright idea of gathering together all the best-known women of the Quarter. The downstairs rooms are full, but the detached wing is free.

KUDAYŪ: Full of cobwebs, no doubt.

MASTER: More of your usual sarcasm, sir?

KUDAYŪ: No, I'm just being careful not to get entangled at my age in a whore's cobweb.

MASTER: I'd never have guessed it. I can't accommodate you downstairs, then. I'll prepare an upstairs room.—Servants! Light the lamps and bring saké and tobacco.

NARRATOR: He calls out in a loud voice. Drums and samisens resound from the back rooms.

KUDAYŪ: What do you think, Bannai? Do you hear how Yuranosuke is carrying on?

BANNAI: He seems completely out of his head. Of course, we've had a series of private reports from you, Kudayū, but not even my master Moronao suspected how far gone Yuranosuke was. Moronao told me to come up to the capital and look over the situation. He said I should report anything suspicious. I'd never have believed it if I hadn't seen it with my own eyes. It's worse than I imagined. And what has become of his son, Rikiya?

KUDAYŪ: He comes here once in a while and the two of them have a wild time together. It's incredible that they don't feel any embarrassment in each other's presence. But to-night I've come with a plan for worming out the inner-most secrets of Yuranosuke's heart. I'll tell you about it when we're alone. Let's go upstairs.

BANNAI: After you.

KUDAYŪ: Well, then, I'll lead the way.

NARRATOR (*sings*):

> Though in truth your heart
> Has no thought for me,
> Your lips pretend you are in love,
> With great bewitchery—

JŪTARŌ: Yagorō and Kitahachi—this is the teahouse where Yuranosuke amuses himself. It's called Ichiriki. Oh, Heiemon, we'll call you when the time comes. Go wait in the kitchen.

HEIEMON: At your service, sir. Please do what you can for me.

JŪTARŌ: Is anyone there? I want to talk to somebody.

MAID: Yes, sir. Who is it, please?

JŪTARŌ: We've come on business with Yuranosuke. Go in and tell him that Yazama Jūtarō, Senzaki Yagorō, and Takemori Kitahachi are here. Several times we've sent a man to fetch him, but he never seems to leave this place. So the three of us have come to him. There's something we must discuss with him. We ask that he meet us. Be sure and tell him that.

MAID: I'm sorry to tell you, sir, but Yuranosuke has been drinking steadily for the past three days. You won't get much sense out of him, even if you see him. He's not himself.

JŪTARŌ: That may be, but please tell him what I said.

MAID: Yes, sir.

JŪTARŌ: Yagorō, did you hear her?

YAGORŌ: I did, and I'm amazed. At first I thought it was some trick of his to throw the enemy off the track. But he has abandoned himself to his pleasures more than convincingly. I simply don't understand it.

KITAHACHI: It's just as I said. He's not the same man in spirit. Our best plan would be to break in on him—

JŪTARŌ: No, first we'll have a heart-to-heart talk.

YAGORŌ: Very well, we'll wait for him here.

PROSTITUTE (*sings*): Come where my hands clap, hands clap, hands clap. (*Yuranosuke enters. He is blindfolded.*)

YURANOSUKE: I'll catch you! I'll catch you!

PROSTITUTE: Come on, Yura the blind man! We're waiting!

YURANOSUKE: I'll catch you and make you drink.—Here!— Now I've got you! We'll have some saké! Bring on the saké! (*He grabs Jūtarō, taking him for his partner in blind-man's buff.*)

JŪTARŌ: Come to yourself, Yuranosuke. I'm Yazama Jūtarō. What in the world are you doing?

YURANOSUKE: Good heavens! What an awful mistake!

PROSTITUTE: Oh, the kill-joys! Look at them, Sakae. Have you ever seen such sour-looking samurai? Are they all in the same party, do you think?

SAKAE: It certainly looks that way. They all have the same fierce look.

JŪTARŌ: Girls, we've come on business with Mr. Ōboshi. We'd appreciate it if you left the room for a while.

PROSTITUTES: We guessed as much. Yura, we'll be going to the back room. Come join us soon. This way, everybody.

JŪTARŌ: Yuranosuke, you remember me. I'm Yazama Jūtarō.

KITAHACHI: I'm Takemori Kitahachi.

YATARŌ: And I am Senzaki Yatarō. We've come here hoping to have a talk with you. I trust you're awake now?

YURANOSUKE: Thank you all for having come to see me. What have you in mind?

JŪTARŌ: When do we leave for Kamakura?

YURANOSUKE: That's a very important question you've asked me. There's a song in *Yosaku from Tamba*[37] that goes, "When you leave for Edo, oh so far away. . . ." Ha, ha. Forgive me, gentlemen, I'm drunk.

THREE MEN: A man's character stays the same even when he's drunk, they say. If you're not in your right mind, the three of us will sober you up.

HEIEMON: Don't do anything rash, please. I hope you'll forgive me, gentlemen, but I'd like a word with him. Please hold off for a while before you start anything. Master Yuranosuke—I am Teraoka Heiemon. I am very glad to see you're in such good spirits.

---

[37] A famous play by Chikamatsu Monzaemon. Cf. Keene, tr., *Major Plays of Chikamatsu*, p. 94.

YURANOSUKE: Teraoka Heiemon? Who might *you* be? Are
  you that fleet-footed foot soldier who was sent as a courier
  to the north?

HEIEMON: The same, sir. It was while I was in the north
  that I learned our master had committed *seppuku*, and I
  was dumfounded. I started off for home, running so fast
  I all but flew through the air. On the way I was told that
  his lordship's mansion had been confiscated and his retainers dispersed. You can imagine what a shock that was.
  I served his lordship only as a foot soldier, but I am as
  much indebted to him as anyone. I went to Kamakura,
  intending to kill Moronao, our master's enemy. For three
  months I watched for my chance, disguising myself as a
  beggar, but our enemy is guarded so strongly I couldn't
  even get close to him. I felt I had no choice but to dis-
  embowel myself, but I thought then of my parents in the
  country, and I went back home, despondent though I was.
  But then—surely it was a heaven-sent revelation—I learned
  about the league you gentlemen have formed. How happy
  and thankful that made me! I didn't even bother to take
  my things with me, but went to call on these gentlemen
  at their lodgings. I begged with all my heart for them to
  intercede in my behalf. They praised me and called me a
  brave fellow, and promised to plead for me with the chief.
  So I've come along with them here, encouraged by their
  assurances. Moronao's mansion—

YURANOSUKE: What's all this? You're not so much light of
  foot as exceedingly light of tongue. It's quite true that I
  felt a certain amount of indignation—about as big as a
  flea's head split by a hatchet—and tried forming a league
  of forty or fifty men, but what a crazy notion that was! I
  realized when I thought about it calmly that if we failed

in our mission our heads would roll, and if we succeeded
we'd have to commit *seppuku* afterwards. Either way, it
was certain death. It was like taking expensive medicine,
then hanging yourself afterwards because you couldn't
pay for the cure. You're a foot soldier with a stipend of
three *ryō* and an allowance of three men's rations. Now
don't get angry—for you to throw away your life attacking
the enemy, in return for a pittance suitable for a beggar
priest, would be like putting on a performance of grand
kagura to express your gratitude for some green *nori*.[38]
My stipened was 1,500 *koku*.[39] Compared to you, I might
take enemy heads by the bushel and still not do my share.
And that's why I gave up the idea. Do you follow me? At
any rate, this uncertain world (*sings*) is just that sort of
place. *Tsuten Tsutsuten Tsutsuten*.[40] Oh, when I hear the
samisens playing like that I can't resist.

HEIEMON: I can't believe that is you speaking, Yuranosuke.
Each man has only one life in this world, whether he's a
wretch like myself with a bare income of three rations,
or a rich man like you with 1,500 *koku*, and there is no
high or low in the debt of gratitude we owe our master.
But there's no disputing family lineage. I know it's presumptuous and rude for a miserable creature like myself
to beg to join distinguished gentlemen who could have
stood as deputies for our master. It's like a monkey imi-

[38] *Kagura* is the sacred music and dance performed at Shinto shrines;
by "grand *kagura*" is meant the especially exalted variety of the Great
Shrine of Ise. Worshipers normally offered performances in return for
blessings received, but a gift of *nori*, a kind of edible seaweed, would
certainly not require such an elaborate display of thanks.

[39] The stipends of samurai were calculated in *koku*, a measure of rice
a little less than five bushels.

[40] Sounds intended to suggest the music of the samisen.

tating a man. But I want to go with you, even if it is only
to carry your shoes or shoulder your baggage. Please take
me with you. Sir, please listen to me, sir.—Oh, he seems
to have fallen asleep.

KITAHACHI: Come, Heiemon. There's no point in wasting any
more breath on him. Yuranosuke is as good as dead. Well,
Yazama and Sensaki, have you see his true character? Shall
we act as we agreed?

YAGORŌ: By all means, as a warning to the others in our
league. Are you ready?

NARRATOR: They close in on Yuranosuke, but a cry from
Heiemon stops them. With calming gestures he comes up
beside them.

HEIEMON: It seems to me, as I turn things over in my mind,
Yuranosuke has undergone many hardships in his efforts to
avenge our master, ever since they were parted by death.
He has had to worry, like a hunted man, over every noise
and footfall, and stifle his resentment at people's abuse.
He couldn't have survived this long if he hadn't taken so
heavily to drink. Wait till he's sober before you deal with
him.

NARRATOR: Forcibly restraining them, he leads them into the
next room. Their shadows on the other side of the sliding
door, cast by a light that illuminates the distinction between good and evil,[41] are blotted out as the moon sinks
behind the mountains.

Rikiya, Yuranosuke's son, having run the whole *ri* and
a half from Yamashina, arrives breathless. He peeps inside

[41] An obscure passage, perhaps intended to suggest that the light dis-
tinguishes these good men from the evil Kudayū, who is lurking in
the next room. The phrase "moon sinks behind the mountains" is used
also to modify the place-name Yamashina in the next line.

and sees his father lying asleep. Afraid that people may hear, he goes up to his father's pillow and rattles his sword in its scabbard, instead of a horse's bit.[42] At the clink of the hilt Yuranosuke suddenly rises.

YURANOSUKE: Is that you, Rikiya? Has something urgent come up? Is that why you rattled the scabbard? Keep your voice low.

RIKIYA: An express courier just brought a secret letter from Lady Kaoyo.

YURANOSUKE: Was there no verbal message besides?

RIKIYA: Our enemy Kō no Moronao's petition to return to his province has been granted and he will shortly start for home. Her ladyship said the details would be found in her letter.

YURANOSUKE: Very good. You return home and send a palanquin for me tonight. Be off now.

NARRATOR: Without a flicker of hesitation Rikiya sets off for Yamashina. Yuranosuke, worried about the contents of the letter, is about to cut the seal when a voice calls.

KUDAYŪ: Master Ōboshi! Master Yuranosuke! It's me, Ono Kudayū. I'd like a word with you.

YURANOSUKE: Well! I haven't seen you in a long time. How wrinkled you've become in the year since we last met. Have you come to this house to unfurrow those wrinkles? What an old lecher you are!

KUDAYŪ: Yura—they say little faults are overlooked in a great achievement. The fast life you've led here in the gay quarters, in defiance of people's criticism, will pave the foundation for your achievements. I consider you a hero, a man of great promise.

[42] Samurai dozing on horseback were said to awaken to the sound of the horse's bit.

YURANOSUKE: Ha, ha. What a hard line you take! You've set up a perfect battery of catapults against me. But let's talk about something else.

KUDAYŪ: There's no point in pretending, Yuranosuke. Your dissipation is, in fact—

YURANOSUKE: You think it's a trick to enable me to attack the enemy?

KUDAYŪ: Of course I do.

YURANOSUKE: How you flatter me! I thought you'd laugh at me as a fool, a madman—over forty and still a slave to physical pleasure. But you tell me it's all a scheme to attack the enemy! Thank you, good Kudayū. You've made me happy.

KUDAYŪ: Then you have no intention of avenging our master Enya?

YURANOSUKE: Not in the least. I know that when we were about to turn over the house and the domain I said I would die fighting in the castle, but that was only to please her ladyship. I remember how you stalked out of the room at the time, saying that resistance would make us enemies of the shogun. But we continued our debate in deadly earnest. What idiots we were! In any case, our discussion got nowhere. We said we'd commit *seppuku* before his lordship's tomb, but one after another we stole out the back gate. I have you to thank for being able to enjoy these pleasures here, and I haven't forgotten our old friendship. Don't act so stiff! Relax with me.

KUDAYŪ: Yes, I see now, when I think back on the old days, that I used to be quite a fraud myself. Shall I show you my true nature and have a drink with you? How about it, Yuranosuke? The first cup we've shared in a long time.

YURANOSUKE: Are you going to ask for the cup back, as at a formal banquet?

KUDAYŪ: Pour the liquor and I'll drink.

YURANOSUKE: Drink up and I'll pour.

KUDAYŪ: Have a full cup. Here, I'll give you something to eat with it.

NARRATOR: He picks up in his chopsticks a piece of octopus that happens to be near him and holds it out to Yuranosuke.

YURANOSUKE: Putting out my hand, I accept an octopus foot. Thank you!

KUDAYŪ: Yuranosuke—tomorrow is the anniversary of the death of our master, Enya Hangan. The night before the anniversary is supposed to be especially important. Are you going to eat that octopus and think nothing of it?

YURANOSUKE: Of course I'll eat it. Or have you had word that Lord Enya has turned into an octopus? What foolish ideas you get into your head! You and I are *rōnin* now, thanks to Lord Hangan's recklessness. That's why I hold a grudge against him. I haven't the faintest intention of becoming a vegetarian for his sake, and I'm delighted to sample the fish you've so kindly provided.

NARRATOR: With the greatest aplomb he gulps down the fish in a single mouthful, a sight that stuns even the crafty Kudayū into silence.

YURANOSUKE: This fish is no good for drinking. We'll get them to wring a chicken's neck and give us chicken in the pot. Let's go to the back room. Come along, girls, and sing for us.

KUDAYŪ (*sings*):

> On uncertain legs he staggers off
> To the lively beat of the samisens
> *Tere tsuku teretsuku tsutsuten tsutsuten* . . .

YURANOSUKE (*to jesters*): Hey, you small fry! Do you expect to be let off without getting soused?

NARRATOR: Amid all the bustle he goes within. Sagisaka Bannai, who has been observing everything from beginning to end, comes down from the second floor.

BANNAI: I've kept close watch on him, Kudayū, and I can't believe a man so rotten at the core he'd even eat animal food on the anniversary of his master's death will ever attack his enemy. I intend to report this to my master Moronao, and to recommend that he relax his precautions and open his gates.

KUDAYŪ: You're right. Lord Moronao need not take such precautions any more.

BANNAI: Look here—he's forgotten his sword!

KUDAYŪ: Yes, that really proves what a nitwit he's become. Let's examine this symbol of his samurai spirit. Why, it's rusty as a red sardine!

BANNAI: Ha, ha, ha!

KUDAYŪ: This certainly shows us his true nature. Your master can set his mind at rest. (*Calls.*) Where are my servants? I'm leaving. Bring my palanquin!

NARRATOR: With a shout they bring it forth.

KUDAYŪ: Now, Bannai, please get in.

BANNAI: No, sir, you're older than I. After you, please.

KUDAYŪ: In that case, by your leave.

NARRATOR: He gets in.

BANNAI: By the way, Kudayū, I hear that Kampei's wife is working in this place. Have you run into her here?

NARRATOR: Surprised not to receive a reply, he lifts the bamboo blinds of the palanquin and sees inside a fair-sized stone.

BANNAI: Good heavens! Kudayū has turned into a stone, like Lady Sayo of Matsuura! [43]

[43] A famous legend, found as early as the *Manyōshū*, tells of this lady

NARRATOR: He looks around him. A voice calls from under the veranda.

KUDAYŪ: Here I am, Bannai. I've played a trick and slipped out of the palanquin. I'm worried about the letter Rikiya brought a while ago. I'll watch what happens and let you know later on. Follow along beside the palanquin. Act as if we were leaving together.

BANNAI: I will.

NARRATOR: He nods in agreement and slowly walks beside the palanquin, pretending someone is inside.

Meanwhile, Kampei's wife Okaru is recovering in her upstairs room from intoxication; familiar now with the Quarter, she lets the blowing breezes dispel her sadness.

YURANOSUKE (*to women in back room*): I'll be back in a moment. Yuranosuke's supposed to be a samurai, but he's forgotten his precious sword. I'll go and fetch it. In the meantime, straighten the kakemono and put some charcoal on the stove.—Oh, I must be careful not to step on that samisen and break it. Well, that's a surprise! It looks as if Kudayū's gone. (*Sings.*)

He hears a tearful voice that cries,
"Father! Mother!" and to his surprise,
The words came from a parrot's beak:
His wife had taught the bird to speak!

NARRATOR: Yuranosuke looks around the room; then, standing under the light of a lantern hanging from the eaves, he reads the long letter from Lady Kaoyo describing in detail the enemy's situation. The letter is in woman's language, full of polite phrases, and not easy to follow.

---

who waved her scarf at the ship carrying her husband to Korea. She waved so long she finally turned to stone. The name Matsuura is sometimes also read Matsura.

Okaru, envious of other people happily in love, tries to read the letter from upstairs, but it is dark and the letter far away and the writing indistinct. It occurs to her that by holding out her mirror to reflect the writing she can read the message. Under the veranda, by the light of the moon, Kudayū reads the letter as it unrolls and hangs, but Yuranosuke, being no god, is unaware of this. Okaru's hair ornament suddenly comes loose and falls. Yuranosuke looks up at the sound and hides the letter behind him. Kudayū, under the veranda, is still in smiles; Okaru in the upstairs room hides her mirror.

OKARU: Is that you, Yura?

YURANOSUKE: Oh, it's you, Okaru. What are you doing there?

OKARU: You got me completely drunk. It was so painful I've been cooling myself in the breeze, trying to sober up.

YURANOSUKE: You're lucky to have such a good breeze. But Okaru, there's a little matter I'd like to discuss with you. I can't talk from here, across the rooftops, like the two stars across the Milky Way—won't you come down here for a moment?

OKARU: Is this matter you'd like to discuss some favor you want to ask me?

YURANOSUKE: Yes, something like that.

OKARU: I'll go around and come down.

YURANOSUKE: No, if you go by the staircase some maid is sure to catch you and make you drink.

OKARU: What shall I do, then?

YURANOSUKE: Look—luckily there's a nine-runged ladder lying here. You can use it to come down.

NARRATOR: He leans the ladder against the eaves of the lower floor.

OKARU: What a funny ladder! Oh, I'm afraid! It feels dangerous somehow.

YURANOSUKE: Don't worry. You're way past the age for feeling afraid or in danger. You could come down three rungs at a time and still not open any new wounds.

OKARU: Don't be silly. I'm afraid. It feels like I'm on a boat.

YURANOSUKE: Of course it does. I can see your little boat god from here.

OKARU: Ohh—you mustn't peep!

YURANOSUKE: I'm admiring the autumn moon over Lake T'ung-t'ing.

OKARU: I won't come down if you're going to act that way.

YURANOSUKE: If you won't come down, I'll knock you up.

OKARU: There you go again with your awful language.

YURANOSUKE: You make such a fuss anybody would think you were a virgin. I'll take you from behind.

NARRATOR: He catches her in his arms from behind and sets her on the ground.

YURANOSUKE: Tell me, did you see anything?

OKARU: No, no, I didn't.

YURANOSUKE: I'm sure you did.

OKARU: It looked like a letter from a girl friend.

YURANOSUKE: Did you read the whole thing from up there?

OKARU: Why are you grilling me so?

YURANOSUKE: It's a matter of life and death.

OKARU: What in the world are you talking about?

YURANOSUKE: I mean—I know it's an old story, Okaru, but I've fallen for you. Will you be my wife?

OKARU: Now stop it! You're lying to me.

YURANOSUKE: The truth may have started as a lie, but if I didn't really mean it, I couldn't go through with it. Say yes, please.

OKARU: No, I won't.

YURANOSUKE: But why?

OKARU: Because what you say is not truth that started as a lie, but a lie that started as truth.

YURANOSUKE: Okaru, I'll redeem your contract.

OKARU: Will you?

YURANOSUKE: I'll prove to you I'm not lying. I'll buy out your contract tonight.

OKARU: No, I have a—

YURANOSUKE: If you have a lover, you can live with him.

OKARU: Do you really mean it?

YURANOSUKE: I swear, by the providence that made me a samurai. As long as I can keep you for three days, you are at liberty to do what you please afterwards.

OKARU: I'm sure you just want me to say how happy I am before you laugh at me.

YURANOSUKE: Absolutely not. I'll give the master the money at once and settle things here and now. You wait here and don't worry about anything.

OKARU: Then I'll wait for you. I promise.

YURANOSUKE: Don't move from the spot until I get back from paying the money. You're my wife now.

OKARU: And for just three days.

YURANOSUKE: Yes, I've agreed.

OKARU: I'm most grateful.

NARRATOR (*sings*):

> If ever woman was born
> Unlucky, I'm the one.
> How many pangs I've suffered
> For the man I love, alas.
> I cry alone with muffled notes
> Like a plover of the night.

Okaru, hearing this song from the back room, is sunk in thought as she feels how closely its words fit herself. At that moment Heiemon suddenly appears.

HEIEMON: Okaru—is that you?

OKARU: Heiemon! How shaming to meet you here!

NARRATOR: She hides her face.

HEIEMON: There's nothing to feel ashamed about. I stopped to see Mother on my way back from the East and she told me everything. It was noble of you to have sold yourself for your husband and our master. I'm proud of you.

OKARU: I am happy if you can think so kindly of me. But I have good news for you. Tonight, most unexpectedly, my contract is to be redeemed.

HEIEMON: No news could please me more. Whom have we to thank for this?

OKARU: Someone you know, Ōboshi Yuranosuke.

HEIEMON: What did you say? Your contract is to be redeemed by Ōboshi Yuranosuke? Have you been intimate with him for a long time?

OKARU: How could I have been? I've occasionally, perhaps two or three times, drunk with him. He said that if I had a husband I could stay with him, and if I wanted to be free he would let me go. It's almost too good to be true.

HEIEMON: You mean, he doesn't know you're married to Hayano Kampei?

OKARU: No, he doesn't. How could I tell him, when my being here is a disgrace to my parents and my husband?

HEIEMON: It would seem, then, he's a libertine at heart. Obviously he has no intention of avenging our master.

OKARU: No, that's not so. He has, I know it. I can't say it aloud, but I'll whisper it. (*Whispers.*)

HEIEMON: Then you definitely saw what the letter said?

OKARU: I read every word. Then we happened to look each other in the face and he began to flirt with me. Finally he talked about redeeming me.

HEIEMON: This was after you read the whole letter?

OKARU: Yes.

HEIEMON: I understand everything, then. My sister, you're doomed. You can't escape. Let me take your life.

NARRATOR: He draws his sword and slashes at her, but she jumps nimbly aside.

OKARU: What is it, Heiemon? What have I done wrong? You're not free to kill me as you please. I have my husband Kampei and both my parents too. I've been looking forward so much to seeing my parents and my husband as soon as my contract is redeemed. Whatever my offense may be, I apologize. Please forgive me, pardon me.

NARRATOR: She clasps her hands in supplication. Heiemon flings down his naked sword and gives way to bitter tears.

HEIEMON: My poor dear sister. I see you know nothing of what happened. Our father, Yoichibei, was stabbed to death by a stranger on the night of the twenty-ninth of the sixth month.

OKARU: It's not possible!

HEIEMON: You haven't heard the worst. You say you want to join Kampei as soon as you're redeemed. But he committed *seppuku* and is dead.

OKARU: Oh, no! Is it true? Tell me!

NARRATOR: She clutches him and, with a cry, collapses in tears.

HEIEMON: I understand. No wonder you cry. But it would make too long a story to tell you everything. I feel sorriest for Mother. Every time she mentions what happened she weeps, every time she remembers she weeps again. She begged me not to tell you, saying you'd cry yourself to death if you knew. I made up my mind not to tell you, but you can't escape death now. Yuranosuke is singlemindedly, fanatically motivated by loyalty. He'd have had no reason to ransom you if he didn't know you were Kampei's wife. Certainly it wasn't because he's infatuated with you. The letter you saw was of the greatest importance. He will redeem your contract only to kill you. I'm sure that's what he has in mind. Even if you tell no one about the letter, the walls have ears, and any word of the plan leaking from somebody else is sure to be blamed on you. You were wrong to have peeped into a secret letter, and you must be killed for it. Rather than let you die at a stranger's hands, I will kill you with my own hands. I can't allow any woman with knowledge of the great secret to escape, even if she's my own sister. On the strength of having killed a person dangerous to our plot I shall ask to join the league and go with the others. The sad thing about being of the lower ranks is that unless you prove to the other samurai your spirit is better than theirs, they won't let you join them. Show you understand by giving me your life. Die for my sake, sister.

NARRATOR: Okaru sobs again and again as she listens to her brother's carefully reasoned words.

OKARU: I kept thinking all the while that the reason why he didn't write me was that he'd used the money I raised as the price of my body and started on his journey. I was resentful because he hadn't even come to say good-by. It's a dreadful thing for me to say, but though Father met a horrible death he was, after all, an old man. But how sad and humiliating it must have been for Kampei to die when he was hardly thirty! I'm sure he must have wanted to see me. Why didn't anyone take me to him? What a terrible fate never even to have abstained from animal food in mourning for my husband and father. What reason have I to go on living? But if I died at your hands I'm sure Mother would hate you for it. I'll kill myself. After I'm dead, if my head or my body can bring you credit, please use it for that purpose. Now I must say farewell to you, my brother.

NARRATOR: She takes up the sword.

YURANOSUKE: Stop! Wait a moment!

NARRATOR: Yuranosuke restrains her. Heiemon jumps in astonishment. Okaru cries out.

OKARU: Let me go! Let me die!

NARRATOR: Yuranosuke holds her back and she struggles, impatient for death.

YURANOSUKE: You are an admirable brother and sister. All my doubts have been resolved. Heiemon, you may join us on our eastward journey. You, Okaru, must live on so you can offer prayers for the future repose of his soul.

OKARU: I'll pray for him by going with him to the afterworld.

NARRATOR: Yuranosuke holds firmly the sword he has twisted from her grasp.

YURANOSUKE: We admitted your husband Kampei to our league, but he was never able to kill a single enemy. What excuse will he be able to offer our master when he meets him in the afterworld? This may serve as his apology!

NARRATOR: He drives the sword hard between the mats. Underneath the floor Kudayū, his shoulder run through, writhes in agony.

YURANOSUKE: Drag him out!

NARRATOR: Even before the command leaves Yuranosuke's

mouth, Heiemon leaps from the veranda and resolutely drags out Kudayū, dripping with blood.

HEIEMON: Kudayū! It serves you right!

NARRATOR: He hauls him up and throws him before Yuranosuke, who grabs Kudayū by the topknot, not letting him rise, and pulls him over.

YURANOSUKE: The worm that feeds on the lion's body—that's you! You received a large stipend from our master and benefited by innumerable other kindnesses, and yet you became a spy for his enemy Moronao and secretly informed him of everything, true and false alike. The forty and more of us have left our parents and separated from our children, and have even forced our wives, who should have been our lifelong companions, to work as prostitutes, all out of the desire to avenge our late master. As soon as we wake up in the morning, then all through the day, we think about how he committed *seppuku,* and the remembrances arouse tears of impotent rage. We have racked ourselves with pain, mind and body. Tonight especially, the night before our master's anniversary, I spoke vile words of every sort, but in my heart I was practicing the most profound abstention. How dared you thrust fish before my face? What anguish I felt in my heart, not being able to accept or refuse. And how do you think I felt on the night before the anniversary of a master whose family my family has served for three generations, when the fish passed my throat? My whole body seemed to crumble to pieces all at once, and my bones felt as though they were breaking. Ahh—you fiend, you diabolical monster!

NARRATOR: He rubs and twists Kudayū's body into the ground, then breaks into tears of despair.

YURANOSUKE: Heiemon, I forgot my rusty sword a while ago. It was a sign I was meant to torture him to death with it. Make him suffer, but don't kill him.

HEIEMON: Yes, sir.

NARRATOR: He unsheathes his sword and at once leaps and pounces on Kudayū, slashing him again and again, though the wounds are superficial. He scores Kudayū's body until no part is left unscathed.

KUDAYŪ: Heiemon, Okaru, please intercede for me!

NARRATOR: He joins his hands in entreaty. What a repulsive sight—Kudayū, who always despised Teraoka as a lowly foot soldier, and refused to favor him with so much as a glance, now prostrates himself humbly.

YURANOSUKE: If we kill him here we'll have trouble explaining it. Pretend he's drunk and take him home.

NARRATOR: He throws his cloak over Kudayū to hide the wounds. Yazama, Senzaki, and Takemori, who have been listening in secret, fling open the sliding doors.

THREE MEN: Yuranosuke, we humbly apologize.

YURANOSUKE: Heiemon—this customer has had too much to drink. Give him some watery gruel for his stomach in the Kamo River.

HEIEMON: Yes, sir.

YURANOSUKE: Go!

Act Eight

The Bridal Journey

NARRATOR: Who was it first spoke of the floating world? Like the pools of Asuka River, the clear sailing of the samurai quickly gives way to shoals, and they become "wave men" with nowhere to turn. Enya's crime has set a weir in the stream of love for the betrothed: Rikiya, the fiancé of Konami, Kakogawa's daughter, refuses now even to accept the engagement presents, and the jilted girl abandons herself to gloomy thoughts; but at her mother's suggestion they set off for Yamashina, counting on the love of Rikiya, the intended bridegroom, to gain them admission to his house. Uncertain whether he will marry her and live up to his obligations or continue to refuse, and fearful of gossip, mother and daughter leave together, taking neither servant nor palanquin, and set their course for the capital. In the cold air Konami's snowy skin is tinged with the color of the winter plum blossom, and her fingertips are numb with chill as they climb Frozen Slope and head for Satta Pass. She looks back and sees the smoke from Fuji disappearing traceless into the sky; her own uncertainty will be dispelled only when she sees the gate fires [44] lit to celebrate her marriage. They pass the pine forest of Miho and next they see along the avenue of pines a great procession that crowds the road. She does not know whose procession this is, but feels envy as she thinks, "If things were as they used to be, I should now be traveling in just such splendor and luxury for the great occasion of my life." They pass Fuchū in Suruga, and when they have left the castle town behind, her mother, to raise their spirits, says cheerfully:

TONASE: Once you've drunk the marriage cups you'll share bedchamber endearments and sweet whisperings that neither your mother nor your child will ever know about, and twined together like the ivy along this road, how happy you'll be!

NARRATOR: She takes the girl by the hand, but Konami at Ball River rolls aside her mother's all too open words. Passing Utsu Mountain she feels at once afraid, ashamed, and happy as she thinks of first sharing in reality her bridegroom's pillow. At Seto the colored rice wafers are crisp, but heavy worries weigh on her as they reach the Ōi River.

KONAMI: They say a man's heart is like a flowing stream. I wonder if his feelings have not changed? Has not some other flower blossomed even in the shade? [45]

NARRATOR: She speaks her thoughts aloud to dispel her fears as they reach Shimada, famed for its coiffure. Nobody knows my griefs, she thinks, as they cross the bridge at Shiratsuka. Further on they hear the voices of the women enticing customers at Yoshida and Akasaka.

[44] Fires were lit at the gate of a bride's house, apparently as a sign she was not to return!

[45] She wonders if Rikiya, despite his having fallen into disfavor (shade), has not found a new sweetheart (flower).

If you'd like a bride,
Visit the Kiyomizu Temple,
Plunge in the Fall of Otowa,
And pray each day for me!
Shishiki gankō gakai rei nyūkyū.[46]

The dancers' drums awaken her from her nap. How she longs to see her sweetheart in the capital and confide to him the pains she's known! "If Mother is there to bring us together, but nobody else, we'll have the Shrine at Ise to thank." Even the rustic songs at Narumi Beach seem a good omen. Is that the Atsuta Shrine over there? The boatman hoists the sail for the seven-mile crossing, and the rowers keep time at their oars. Is the creak of the rudder a bell cricket? No, it's a grasshopper that chirps this frosty night, as in the old poem.[47]

TONASE: That poem tells of a scene late at night, but we have only till dusk to catch the last boat. We must hurry.

NARRATOR: When the mother runs, the daughter runs too. Hail falls from the sky and they cover their heads with wicker hats. The passengers on the boat they met now pass them on the road, now fall behind. They go by Shōno, Kameyama, and stop at Seki where the road forks between Ise and the East. They cross Suzuka Pass, where the bell of the imperial messenger still rings. At "Tsuchi-yama in between the rain is falling," [48] everybody says at Minakuchi. At the quarry in Ishibe she gathers big stones

---

[46] This Buddhist-sounding incantation has been interpreted as a phrase descriptive of sexual intercourse.

[47] Reference to the poem, no. 518 in *Shin Kokin Shū*, by Fujiwara Yoshitsune: "How the grasshoppers are chirping! Will I have to sleep alone this frosty night, my cloak spread over my cold mat?"

[48] See Keene, tr., *Major Plays of Chikamatsu*, p. 103. This was part of a ballad incorporating the names of famous places along the Tōkaidō.

and small stones and rubs them in her hands because
they remind her of her husband [49]—may they soon meet!
Next they pass Ōtsu and cross beneath the foot of the
Miidera, and now they hurry on to Yamashina, not far
away.

[49] Ōishi (big stone) was the real name of Ōboshi Rikiya. See Introduction, p. 5.

Act Nine

NARRATOR: Yamashina has neither elegance nor fashion nor anything else to recommend it, but here Yuranosuke has his lonely house. He spent last night at the teahouse in Gion, detained by the snow, and returns home this morning, accompanied on the way by jesters and waitresses. Frolicsome with drink, he tries to roll a snowball, but instead of rolling snow he is rolled in snow himself, antics that do no credit to his station in life.

JESTER: Master, excuse me, master, but you certainly have a fine view from your parlor. And the bamboos in your garden weighed down with snow look just like a picture. It's lovely, isn't it, Oshina?

OSHINA: Yes, when I look at this view I don't feel like going anywhere else.

YURANOSUKE: Don't you know the poem, "When you see them day and night they lose their charms—the mountains of Awaji Island across the sea from Sumiyoshi"? [50] A man can't drink at home, no matter how proud he is of his garden. You're not very clever, are you? Come, let's go

[50] Slightly misquoted from a poem in *Shin Go Shūi Shū*.

129

in. I wonder where my wife has gone, just when I have guests.

NARRATOR: He leads the way, following the stepping stones on legs as uncertain as his speech, all too obviously drunk. His wife Oishi guesses from the noise that he has returned and lightly comes forward with tea more fragrant than any prepared in a teahouse, for the flavor is imparted by her gentle spirit.

OISHI: You must be cold!

NARRATOR: Her words of solicitude betray no tinge of jealousy. She offers a cup of salt-tea [51] to sober him, but after drinking one mouthful he empties the rest.

YURANOSUKE: What an insensitive woman to have for a wife! Imagine trying to sober me, just when I'm feeling good! Ahh, look how the snow has fallen! [52] I'm sure these people must think you're jealous. Snow, they say, is like whipped cotton—once it flies it turns into padding. And once a wife gets to be called "mama" she becomes nothing but a drudge. Please pardon the lateness of my visit to your private parts, madame. It would appear that unless lobsters, saké cups, and the fence round the Inari Shrine in the Grotto [53] are red people will lose their faith. Oh! I've got a kink in my thigh and I've sprained my big toe. That's better now. While I'm about it, this is what I'll do.

NARRATOR: He pokes her with his foot.

OISHI: Stop your clowning, please, and behave yourself. You

[51] Ordinary tea (bancha) to which salt has been added; it was believed to be effective in sobering someone who was intoxicated.

[52] The following lines are derived from a passage in the Nō play Hachinoki. Cf. Arthur Waley, tr., The Nō Plays of Japan, p. 101.

[53] The Ana (Grotto) Inari Shrine was in Ueno, Edo.

talk such nonsense when you've had too much to drink. (*To others.*) I'm sure he's been a great nuisance.

NARRATOR: She gently tends him. Rikiya, who understands his father's intent, comes in from the back.

RIKIYA: Excuse me, Mother, but has Father gone to sleep? Please give him this.

NARRATOR: He holds out a pillow of lacquered paulownia wood: though father and son act differently, at heart they are moved by the same sense of loyalty. Yuranosuke mutters something, in dream or in reality?

OISHI (*to jesters and waitresses*): Will you please all leave now?

JESTERS: Yes, we will, we will. Give our best regards to your husband when he wakes up. And young master, do come and pay us a little visit.

NARRATOR: With winks they make their unseemly departure. Yuranosuke waits until they are beyond earshot, then lifts his head from the pillow.

YURANOSUKE: Rikiya, do you know what I had in mind when I rolled this snowball, pretending to be drunk?

RIKIYA: Snow as it falls is so light the least gust of wind scatters it, but when you roll it into a ball it becomes strong as a rock. Even boulders can be smashed when a snowstorm blows down from the peak. Loyalty is a heavy responsibility. But even the snow you have rolled into a ball, with all the weightiness of loyalty in your mind, will melt if kept too many days. Was that your meaning?

YURANOSUKE: No, you haven't understood me. You and I, Hara Gōemon, and all the others of the forty-seven in our league, are masterless outcasts living under a shadow. Snow won't melt as long as it is kept in the shadows, and

that is a sign we must not be too hasty. The snowball is
lying in the sunlight now—put it in the yard behind
the house. The stories they tell of men who collected
fireflies or piled up snow to read at night by the reflected
light are meant to show the patience of the scholars. (*To
the serving women.*) Open the small gate from the inside.
I must write a letter to someone in Sakai.[54] Let me know
when the messenger arrives.

MAIDS: Yes, sir.

NARRATOR: They push the snowball through the gate into
the back yard, then shut the door. The sliding doors are
opened and all go inside.

A visitor comes now to this obscure retreat in Yamashina, a place as hard to fathom as the depths of a human
heart; it is Tonase, the wife of Kakogawa Honzō Yukikuni.
She orders the palanquin she rode in, to help find the way,
to wait nearby; then all alone, two swords girded at her
side, perfect in her bearing as always, she goes to the
cottage door and asks to be admitted. At her voice a maid
comes flying out, slipping off the cord she used to tie
back her sleeves. In the old days a page would have performed this service for visitors to Ōboshi's house, but now
it is the maid Rin. "Who's there?" she calls in strident
tones.

TONASE: Is this the house of Mr. Ōboshi Yuranosuke? If so,
would you inform him that Tonase, the wife of Kakogawa
Honzō, is here. We have really been quite out of touch
lately, and I've traveled all this way to consult him about
a certain matter.

NARRATOR: Having sent this message inside, she goes to the

---

[54] We soon discover that the recipient is the merchant Gihei. Sakai
was celebrated as a commercial city and port.

gate and directs the bearers to bring the palanquin closer. She calls her daughter, and Konami emerges, her face wreathed in smiles like a song thrush that discovers flowering plum blossoms as it flies into a valley. She wears her head covering [55] far down over her face.

KONAMI: Is this Rikiya's house already? I feel so embarrassed.

NARRATOR: How charming she is! The maid, having tidied the room, addresses them.

RIN: The master asks you please to come in.

TONASE: Bearers, you may leave. (*To Rin.*) Please show us in.

NARRATOR: The girl Konami, in high spirits, follows her mother in. When they have seated themselves Oishi composedly enters and welcomes them.

OISHI: What an unexpected pleasure! How kind of you both to have come! I should have long since gone to offer my respects. It embarrasses me to be favored by a visit, considering our present circumstances, which no doubt you've heard about.

TONASE: You speak like a stranger. It's true we are meeting today for the first time, but ever since I promised my daughter Konami to your son Rikiya you and I have been in-laws, haven't we? We needn't stand on ceremony, need we?

OISHI: How kind of you to say so. I never expected that anyone as busy as Honzō's wife would visit Kyoto in this cold weather. Perhaps you've been here before, Tonase, but I'm sure Konami must find the capital quite exciting. Have you seen Gion, Kiyomizu, the Chion-in, and the Great Buddha? If you'd like to visit the Golden Pavilion I can get you an introduction.

[55] She is wearing a *wata-bōshi*, the traditional hat for a bride.

NARRATOR: Konami, too shy to lift her head, can only murmur a timid assent to these unconstrained remarks. Tonase sits more formally.

TONASE: I'll tell you why we've come today. After I had already promised my daughter here to your son, that unexpected tragedy struck your master Lord Enya, and ever since then we have lost all track of Yuranosuke and Rikiya. Change, they say, is the way of the world, but a mother's heart never changes. I enquired here and there and learned that you were living here in Yamashina. I was so anxious to give you my daughter in marriage, now that she's of the proper age, that I have burst in on you in this most presumptuous manner. My husband should also have come, but his official duties give him no respite. These two swords are my husband's soul, and when I wear them I speak for us both, for I serve as his deputy. I should like to see Yuranosuke too. It will be a great load off my mind when the wedding has finally been celebrated. Fortunately, this is a lucky day in the calendar. I hope you will be so kind as to make preparations for the ceremony.

OISHI: I hadn't expected such a request. I am sorry that my husband is out, but I am sure that if he were at home and saw you he would answer, "I am deeply grateful for your kindness. When the engagement was arranged I was still in my late master's service and receiving a stipend from him. I asked Honzō for his daughter and he consented. A promise was made. But now I am a *rōnin*, without even a servant, and despite the promises we may have made, the daughter of a high-ranking officer like Kakogawa would make as ill-suited a bride for my son as, to use the vulgar expression, a paper lantern for a temple bell. When the parties are so badly matched there can be no marriage. It isn't as if we had already exchanged engagement gifts. Please give your daughter in marriage to anyone else you wish, without any hesitation." That is what he would say.

NARRATOR: Tonase is startled by these words, but she persists.

TONASE: I gather from your words, Oishi, although you speak so humbly, you believe the positions of Honzō and Yuranosuke are incompatible. If that is the case, please let me speak my mind. My husband's master is a minor noble, so Honzō receives a mere 500 *koku* as his senior retainer. Lord Enya was a daimyo and his chief retainer, Yuranosuke, enjoyed a stipend of 1,500 *koku*. This means, doesn't it, that you agreed to the marriage even though there was a difference in income of 1,000 *koku?* Now your husband is a *rōnin*, but even if everything has been taken away the difference between his income and Honzō's is only 500 *koku*.

OISHI: No, you miss the point. There's no reason why my son couldn't marry a great lord's daughter, even if the difference in income was 10,000 *koku* and not merely 500, provided there was a true matching of hearts.

TONASE: Let me ask you this, Oishi. When you speak of a matching of hearts, whose hearts are you referring to?

OISHI: Our master Lord Enya Hangan died by his own hand. This was because of his hasty temper, it is true, but the tragedy arose from his uncompromising honesty. It was quite a different matter with Honzō, who used gold and silver to curry favor with Moronao. The precious son of Yuranosuke, a man who refuses to serve two masters, cannot take a wife so ill-suited as the daughter of Honzō, a man who draws a stipend as a sycophant samurai.

NARRATOR: Tonase rises at these words.

TONASE: A sycophant samurai? Whom do you mean by that? I refuse to let such an insult go unanswered. I've already endured enough insults because of love for my daughter. A wife is bound, in any case, to defer to her husband. But whether or not there's a formal marriage ceremony, in the eyes of the world Konami has been Rikiya's wife ever since their engagement.

OISHI: Most interesting. If she's his wife, her husband divorces her. As Rikiya's mother, acting on his behalf, I divorce her.

NARRATOR: With this declaration, proof of how far apart their hearts are, she flings open the sliding doors and goes inside. The girl bursts into tears.

KONAMI: Rikiya and I were engaged because we loved each other, and I came here, trusting in your promise that you would bring us together. But instead I am to be divorced by my cruel mother-in-law. I can't think what I've done to deserve this. Please, Mother, apologize for me, and let us have the wedding.

NARRATOR: She clings to her mother and weeps. Tonase gazes long into her daughter's face.

TONASE: It may be a mother's partiality, but I think my daughter is prettier than most. I was anxious to find the right husband for you, and it was after careful consideration that I chose Rikiya. But our journey has been in vain. Imagine Oishi divorcing you without even consulting your husband! That goes quite beyond a mother's duties. I've never heard the like—a mother-in-law divorcing her son's wife. (*Reflects.*) Ah-ha. I have it. Now that he is a *rōnin* with no one to depend on, Rikiya has profited by his distinguished lineage to marry some rich merchant's daughter. He's lost all sense of duty and propriety. Come,

Konami. The man's character is no better than I've described it. If he's divorced you, why don't you spite him? I'm sure plenty of other men would be delighted to have you. Isn't there anyone else you'd like to marry? I'm asking a serious question. I want a definite answer and no weeping. What do you say?

NARRATOR: The mother's nerves are stretched taut as a bow.

KONAMI: What a cruel thing to say, Mother! When we left home Father said, "I've been lucky in my choice of a son-in-law. Ōboshi Rikiya is only a *rōnin*, but he is outstanding in conduct and ability. A chaste wife does not marry a second time. Even if you should leave this husband you must never marry again. That would be the same as infidelity in a married woman. Never forget, whether awake or asleep, to hold your husband in high honor, and be a good daughter in every way to Yuranosuke and his wife. No matter how close you and your husband may be, you must never, not even in a joke, display any jealousy, for that will lead to divorce. And when you are with child, let me know at once. Don't conceal it for fear of worrying me." These were his words and I remember them perfectly. If I go home, a divorced woman, I shall make Father suffer more than ever. Say what you will, whatever reasons there may be, I refuse to marry anyone but Rikiya. I refuse.

NARRATOR: When she hears her daughter express this unswerving resolve to remain true to her love, Tonase can endure no more. Overcome with tears, she determinedly unsheathes her sword.

KONAMI: Mother, what are you doing?

NARRATOR: At these words of restraint Tonase lifts her head.

TONASE: How can you ask such a question? Yes, it's just as

you said, your father would like the marriage celebrated as soon as possible. He's anxious to see the face of his first grandchild and, like all fathers, he dotes on his daughter. How can I go back with you and tell him, when he is so happy, that you were divorced and sent back even before you were married? But, if your mother-in-law rejects you, there is nothing I can do. It is especially humiliating for me because you are not my child but Honzō's by a previous marriage, and he may wonder if I neglected you for that reason. I can't go on living if he suspects that of me. I have no choice. When I am dead please tell your father what I have said, and beg his forgiveness.

KONAMI: You shouldn't say such things. I don't deserve it. I'm the one who should die—my husband hates me. What an ingrate I am to make you suffer this way after all your kindness! Please, Mother, kill me with your own hands. Even though I have been rejected, I will die happy if I can die here, in my husband's house. Please, kill me, quickly.

TONASE: You've spoken well. I'm proud of you. Yes, I will kill you, but not you alone. I will accompany you on the road of death. I will kill you with my own hands, then follow you at once. Are you ready?

NARRATOR: Bravely holding back the tears, she slowly rises.

TONASE: Konami, listen! Do you hear the komusō [56] at the gate playing his flute? That song is "The Cranes in Their Nest." Even birds love their young—what terrible crossing of fates has made me slay with my own hands a blameless child?

---

[56] A variety of Zen priest who goes begging from door to door. His face is almost completely concealed by the basket he wears over his head. He plays the shakuhachi, a kind of bamboo flute.

NARRATOR: At the thought her legs all but give way. At last she lifts the sword in her trembling hands. Konami sits bravely underneath it, her hands joined in prayer.

KONAMI: Hail Amida Buddha!

NARRATOR: Even as she pronounces the invocation a voice shouts, "Stop!" and the strength goes from Tonase's hands before she realizes it. The flute falls silent at the same moment.

TONASE: Oh, it must have been the *komusō*'s flute they were stopping. I so desperately want to spare you that I faltered when the voice called, "Stop!" Don't laugh at me for my weakness. Daughter, are you ready?

NARRATOR: Again she lifts the sword, again the flute begins to play, and at that instant the voice again calls, "Stop!"

TONASE: Does that voice mean there are no alms for the priest? Or is it meant to restrain my uplifted hand?

VOICE: I stopped the hand with the sword. I'll let my son Rikiya marry your daughter.

TONASE: That's Oishi's voice! Do you mean it? Is it true?

NARRATOR: From beyond the sliding doors they hear a voice singing a felicitous passage from Nō.

VOICE: "The two pines that grow from a single trunk make a truly auspicious sight." [57]

NARRATOR: Oishi comes out bearing at a height a little below eye-level a small stand of plain wood.

OISHI: Your determination, Tonase, has touched me. You were ready to kill your only daughter, though you're bound to her by ties of obligation. And you, Konami, showed true chastity. Out of pity for you both, I will

[57] A passage from the Nō play *Takasago*, considered highly felicitous and therefore suitable for singing at weddings.

permit the marriage, though it goes against me. In return, I should like a rather unusual pledge from the bride, on this stand, if you are prepared to give it.

NARRATOR: Oishi puts down the stand. Tonase, somewhat reassured, restores her drawn sword to its sheath.

TONASE: An unusual pledge? I suppose you mean you'd like a dowry present. These two swords have been passed down in my husband's family for generations. The big one is a Masamune, the dagger is a Naminohira Yukiyasu.[58] These heirlooms, that cannot be bought for house or life, I offer as our bridal gifts.

NARRATOR: Oishi interrupts.

OISHI: A fine present to offer a son-in-law—as much as to say you despise him for being *rōnin* and are giving him two valuable swords so he can sell them if ever he's desperate. That's not what I want.

TONASE: Then what do you want?

OISHI: The head of Kakogawa Honzō, on this wooden stand.

TONASE: His head! But why?

OISHI: Our master Lord Enya Hangan, in his anger at Kō no Moronao, slashed him with his sword at the Kamakura Palace. Your husband, Kakogawa Honzō, happening to be present at the time, caught our master in his arms and held him back. That was the only reason why Lord Enya was unable to exact vengeance. His enemy escaped with just a slight wound, but his lordship was obliged to commit *seppuku*, to no purpose. He said nothing at the time,

---

[58] Masamune was probably the most famous of all swordsmiths. He lived in the early part of the fourteenth century. Naminohira Yukiyasu, another great swordsmith, is said to have lived during the reign of the Emperor Ichijō (980–1011).

but how his sense of outraged pride must have made him
hate Honzō! Could he have felt otherwise? If you think
that Rikiya, his retainer, is the kind of man who could
calmly take to wife the daughter of that selfsame Kakogawa, and you still wish to go through with the marriage,
I want Honzō's white head on this stand. If you refuse,
my husband and I will put other heads there, it doesn't
matter whose.[59] We'll have the marriage ceremony just
as soon as we have seen Honzō's head. What do you say?
Is it yes or no? I want your answer!

NARRATOR: With sharp words she relentlessly drives home
her argument. Mother and daughter bow their heads,
at a loss for words, when a voice calls.

HONZŌ: I offer you the head of Kakogawa Honzō. Please
take it.

NARRATOR: The *komusō* who had been standing at the gate
removes his hat and throws it down. He silently walks
inside.

KONAMI: Father!

TONASE: Honzō, what are you doing here? And in that disguise? I don't understand. What does it mean?

NARRATOR: His wife reproves him.

HONZŌ: Don't make such a fuss. It's undignified. I've heard
every word. I'll tell you later how I managed to get here
without letting you know. But, for the moment, keep still.
(*To Oishi.*) I gather you are Oishi, Yuranosuke's wife. I
am Kakogawa Honzō. I imagined something of this sort
might happen and I decided, without telling my wife
and daughter, to have a look for myself. Just as I expected,

---

[59] It is not clear what Oishi is threatening to do. Perhaps she means
that if she can't get Honzō's head she and her husband will offer the
heads of Tonase and Konami to appease the spirit of Enya Hangan.

you want my head as a bridal dowry for the groom. Ha, ha. Those are words fit for a samurai. But your husband is leading the life of a debauchee, with no thought of avenging his master. He has given himself to pleasure and he drinks so heavily it's enough to disorder his senses. He's a model lunatic for all Japan, and Rikiya—tadpoles turn into frogs, as they say—is just as big a fool as his father. The dull sword of a cowardly samurai will never cut off Honzō's head. Enough of this nonsense!

NARRATOR: He tramples on the stand and shatters it.

HONZŌ: That broken-down ex-samurai! I refuse to have such a son-in-law, you impudent hussy!

NARRATOR: She does not let him finish.

OISHI: That's going too far, Honzō! I'll show you whether or not a *rōnin's* rusty sword will still cut. I'm unworthy of him, but I'm Yuranosuke's wife. You're an opponent after my heart. Come, let's have it out!

NARRATOR: She tucks up the hems of her skirts and, snatching a lance from its rack on the wall, readies herself for an attack. Tonase and Konami rush up to stop and separate them.

TONASE *and* KONAMI: Don't be so rash! Wait!

HONZŌ: Out of my way!

NARRATOR: He roughly brushes them aside. At once Oishi thrusts the lance at him. He grabs it by the socket and twists the point away. She turns her back, then springs on him, intending to run through his legs. He kicks upward at the back of the blade and it drops from her hands. She runs up, desperate lest he take the lance, but he catches her by the waist and sash and, pushing her down, holds her there motionless, his knee on her. Honzō is implacable, and Oishi, prostrate beneath him, gnashes her teeth in helpless rage. As Tonase and Konami watch in terror, Ōboshi Rikiya rushes up and, before anyone even notices him, takes up the fallen lance and drives it into Honzō's right side, piercing through to the left. Honzō falls on his face with a groan. Tonase and Konami cry out in despair and cling to him, lamenting, but Rikiya, taking no notice of them, pulls out the lance and prepares to deliver a final thrust. (*Yuranosuke suddenly enters.*)

YURANOSUKE: Stop! Control yourself, Rikiya!

NARRATOR: Yuranosuke, holding back the lance, turns to the wounded man.

YURANOSUKE: It's been a long time since we last met, Honzō. Your plan has worked. You've been struck down by your son-in-law's hand, as you intended. I trust you're satisfied.

NARRATOR: Honzō's eyes widen with surprise at Ōboshi's astuteness.

HONZŌ: What patient care you have given to planning your vengeance for your master's wrongs, even meeting your enemies in the brothels to put them off guard. I am sure your fellow conspirators are all lined up now.—But when I think of it, I should by rights be in your position. Last spring, at the consecration of the Tsurugaoka Shrine, my master Momonoi Wakasanosuke was insulted by Kō no Moronao and enraged beyond measure. He sent for me privately and disclosed what had happened. The expression on his face told me he had made up his mind to confront Moronao in the palace the following day and cut him down with his sword. There was no way to restrain his youthful hot temper. I was sure that my master had been humiliated because the bribes our limited means permitted were insufficient, and Moronao had been annoyed. So I went to Moronao, without telling my master, and offered him presents of gold, silver, and clothing, far beyond our means, and I flattered him, though my words offended me. All this I did because of my love for my master. The bribe was successful and Moronao apologized. This made my master waver, and being unable to kill him, despite his intentions, his resentment melted away. That day Moronao's anger shifted, and Lord Enya suffered instead. I held him back because I supposed he would not have to commit *seppuku* as long as his enemy did not die. My calculations went too far. It was the worst mistake of my life, but I never thought it would cause such grief to my daughter. I decided to offer my gray head to my son-in-law, and sent my wife and daughter to the capital ahead of me. I begged to be dismissed from my master's service, accusing myself of having toadied to Moronao. By taking a different route I arrived at the capital two days before them. The flute-playing I learned when I was young stood me in good stead, and for the past four days I have observed you and seen through your intentions. If I die at your hands, it will appease your resentment, and if you join my daughter with Rikiya, as you promised, I will never forget your kindness through all ages to come. See, I join my hands in supplication. This life, which I never thought I would give up except in my master's service, I yield for my child. Yura, show you understand what it means to be a parent.

NARRATOR: His voice is choked with tears. His wife and daughter are beside themselves.

KONAMI: We had not the least suspicion of this. It's too painful to think you are giving up your life only because

we were so slow in killing ourselves! What terrible punishment from the gods awaits us! Forgive us, Father!

NARRATOR: She falls to the ground weeping and grieving.
Ōboshi, his wife, and his son bow their heads in sympathy.

YURANOSUKE: Honzō, they say that the superior man hates
the crime, but not the offender.[60] I am sure you are angry
with me for not having treated as quite separate matters
your daughter's marriage and our personal grudge. But
since you must shortly depart this world let me reveal to
you the secret of my heart.

NARRATOR: He flings open the sliding doors of the back
garden to reveal the two grave monuments he has fashioned of packed snow, anticipating what will happen;
they foretell his son's end and his own.

NARRATOR: Tonase is quick to grasp the meaning.

TONASE: The snow signifies your intention of melting away
and not serving a second master, once you have avenged
your late lord. Rikiya, with the same thought, divorced my
daughter, a cruelty born of great pity. It makes me sad,
Oishi, to think I was angry with you.

OISHI: Yes, that is so, Tonase. We took into our house a
bride destined to become a widow, a bride we could not
wish the long years of flowering of the jewel-camellia.[61]
Nothing could be at once so joyous and so sad. I spoke
to you cruelly and unfeelingly because I wanted to avoid
such a wedding. How you must have hated me!

[60] A saying, attributed to Confucius, found in the Sung collection
K'ung Ts'ung Tzu.

[61] A reference to a passage in Chuang Tzu: "Long, long ago there was a
great rose of Sharon that counted eight thousand years as one spring
and eight thousand years as one autumn" (Burton Watson, tr., Complete Works of Chuang Tzu, p. 30).

TONASE: No, it is I who feel ashamed and sad. To think that in my anger I should have wondered if Rikiya had married the daughter of a merchant family and forgotten duty and propriety! I cannot hold up my head for shame, Oishi.

OISHI: Why, Tonase, should a girl superior to most in both birth and beauty have been born to such an unhappy fate?

NARRATOR: Her voice is choked with tears. Honzō, holding back his hot tears, speaks.

HONZŌ: I am happy. Everything has turned out as I hoped. The loyalty of Wu Tzu-hsü, who laughed at disgrace when executed for having remonstrated with the King of Wu,[62] no longer merits our attention. Our models of loyalty will be Yu Jang in China [63] and Ōboshi in Japan. From ancient times to the present, in China and Japan, there have been only these two men. To have become the wife of Rikiya, the son of one of these men, is a hundred times better for a samurai's daughter than to have been chosen to share the emperor's bed. Konami, you have proved your worth. (*To Rikiya.*) And now let me present the bridegroom of my worthy daughter with the list of gifts.

NARRATOR: He takes out the list. Rikiya respectfully lifts it to his forehead and opens it.

RIKIYA: What's this? It's not a list—it's a plan of Moronao's mansion! Yes, here's the entrance, the living quarters, the guardroom, the water gate, the storehouses, and even the woodshed, all drawn in detail!

NARRATOR: Yuranosuke respectfully takes it in his hands.

---

[62] See Burton Watson, tr., *Records of the Grand Historian of China*, II, 373.

[63] A famous minister of the Chin dynasty who, out of loyalty to his master, unsuccessfully attempted a vendetta against his master's enemy.

YURANOSUKE: I am deeply grateful. The members of our league have all been chosen, but we have delayed starting because we didn't know the layout of the enemy's place. This plan will be for us like the secret books of Sun Tzu and Wu Tzu or the *Liu Tao* and *San Lüeh*.[64] We've already decided on a night attack. We'll get over the wall with jointed ladders. Then, to break secretly into the house, we need only remove the shutters. This passage leads directly into the sitting room. We'll cut it off here, and attack this way.

NARRATOR: Father and son rejoice, but Honzō is still alert, despite his wounds.

HONZŌ: No, that would be a mistake. Kō no Moronao has taken extreme precautions. The outside and inside sliding doors are all reinforced from behind, and the shutters are bolted together. You can't twist them open, and smashing them with sledge hammers would make a noise and alert the guards. What do you plan to do?

YURANOSUKE: I've thought of a way of dealing with that. Too much absorption with a problem blocks one's thought, they say, but here is the plan I conceived when I was on my way back from the gay quarters: I remembered the bamboos weighted with snow in my garden, and they suggested to me how to get rid of the shutters. I'll show you how it works.

NARRATOR: He jumps down into the garden, where a great, strong bamboo stands, bent under the weight of the deep fall of snow. He twists it round and, bending it like a bow, inserts the tip under the lintel.

---

[64] Sun Tzu and Wu Tzu were Chinese masters of military strategy, and their writings were often consulted for guidance. *Liu Tao* and *San Lüeh* are the names of textbooks of military science.

YURANOSUKE: We'll make bows like this and fit strings to them. Then we'll put the end between the lintels and the frames. When we cut the strings all at once, this is what will happen.

NARRATOR: He shakes the snow from the branch and, as it falls, the bamboo straightens of itself with its innate strength. The lintel bends and the sliding doors, forced from their grooves, clatter down one after the other. Honzō, forgetting his pain, exclaims.

HONZŌ: Splendid! With such a resourceful and loyal retainer Lord Enya should have been more prudent. What a rash and unfortunate way to have behaved!

NARRATOR: Hearing these words of regret, Yuranosuke recalls his master's quick-tempered action, and in his heart he chokes with impotent rage that he never had the chance to display his loyalty on the battlefield, going before his master's horse; tears alone escape the portals of his heart. Rikiya silently goes down into the garden and bows before his father, his hands on the ground.

RIKIYA: Now that we know the layout of our enemy's house, thanks to Honzō's kindness, I will get in touch with Amakawaya Gihei at Sakai in the province of Izumi, and make arrangements for the equipment to be sent.

NARRATOR: Yuranosuke interrupts.

YURANOSUKE: How can you propose that? Everybody knows that Yuranosuke is in Yamashina. It will attract attention if we gather our people here. We should proceed first to Sakai, and from there start on our journey immediately. You remain here with your mother, your wife, and Tonase and take care of any unfinished business. Make sure that you leave nothing to regret. Do you follow me? Take the boat down to Sakai tomorrow night. As for me, Honzō's disguise will come in handy.

NARRATOR: He throws the priest's robe over his shoulders and puts on the wicker hat. Grateful for the kindness he has received, and eager to dispel Honzō's uncertainty about the future,[65] Yuranosuke compassionately grants the bride this one night of love. As he sets out he moistens the mouthpiece of his flute and begins to play the "Song of Love." Oishi has been resigned to his departure, but still she is grief-stricken. All she can say is, "May you have success!" How pathetic that she cannot speak the many words of sorrow over parting! The wounded man knows his last moments have come, but in his final agony cannot reply when his daughter calls to him. The ties binding father and child are snapped with the thread of his life; mother and daughter weep at this sad and final parting.[66] They intone together, mourners and lovers, the Invocation to the Buddha, praying for the repose of the dead man. Yuranosuke's feet pause as he starts to leave, but he plays with the sounds of his flute the six words of the Invocation: Na Mu A Mi Da Butsu. The flute tells of the 108 sources of suffering in this dream life; even as they pray for the dead man's salvation, they know in their hearts that the young couple's happiness, which brings him solace, will last but a single night. Leaving this regret behind, Yura starts off on his journey.

[65] The meaning is somewhat ambiguous, but presumably Honzō is anxious to have his daughter officially accepted as Rikiya's bride; otherwise, he will not have any peace in the life to come.

[66] It was believed that the ties of parent and child lasted for only one lifetime; those of husband and wife lasted for two lifetimes; and those of master and vassal for three.

Act Ten

NARRATOR: Sakai is a great port, the biggest in the world, the center of trade for Settsu, Izumi, and Kawachi, with ships going to foreign countries too. And in Sakai, this town of clever merchants, lives Amakawaya Gihei, a man of unblemished reputation who has steadily amassed a fortune. He lives unassumingly but, though no one would guess it, is a man of substantial means. He is in his shop now, tying heavy boxes with his own hands. The captain of a large ship addresses him.

CAPTAIN: This makes just seven cases I've received.

NARRATOR: His men, shouldering the boxes on poles, go off into the twilight. The master of the shop heaves a sigh of relief.

GIHEI: The weather is good. You should have fine sailing.

NARRATOR: He lights a pipe of tobacco, puffing on it as he goes inside. His son and heir, just turned four this year, is watched over by a round-faced boy of nineteen [67] who is more a playmate than a guardian.

IGO: The performance is about to begin! What fun! *The*

[67] Ages are given in the Japanese style; he would be seventeen or eighteen by Western reckoning.

Wife of Shinoda, as played by Benkei the Weeper.[68] Ladies and gentlemen! We are about to present the heart-rending story of Yoshimatsu. The poor child's mother has been divorced and sent away, and he has only his father now. That's why he's called Benkei the Weeper.

YOSHIMATSU: I'm tired of puppet shows, Igo. I want my mother.

IGO: If you're going to talk like a spoiled brat I'll tell the master and he'll get rid of you too. First the master and his missus split last month. Then he chased out the clerk, saying he was blind as a newborn mouse. And the cook was fired for having given a big yawn. The only ones left now are you, me, and the master. In the end I suppose we'll all be sneaking out of the house. Box after box of our belongings keeps going off to the ship. If we're going to run away, let's take the puppets with us.

YOSHIMATSU: I'd rather sleep than look at your puppet shows any more.

IGO: Are you trying to entice me? Well, if you insist, I'll take you in my arms and sleep with you.

YOSHIMATSU: No, I don't want to.

IGO: Why not?

YOSHIMATSU: You won't give me any milk. I don't want you.

IGO: There you go with your unreasonable talk again. If you were a girl I'd give you something better than milk. But there's no helping it—we're both men. That's something else to weep about.

NARRATOR: Just then two samurai appear at the gate.

SAMURAI: Excuse us, but is Master Gihei at home?

NARRATOR: The man's voice is low, but it has an edge.

---

68 *The Wife of Shinoda* (*Shinoda-zuma*) was an old *jōruri* play, very tearful in content. A "weeping Benkei" generally means a sore loser.

IGO: The master's inside. We've got our hands full with our puppet show. Go right in if you have business with him.

SAMURAI: No, it wouldn't be polite to go in without having ourselves announced. Please tell him Hara Gōemon and Ōboshi Rikiya would like to see him privately.

IGO: What's that? Hara Heriemon? [69] What a glutton you must be! That's terrible! Master! Some great big strangers have come!

NARRATOR: Shouting in this way, he goes inside with Yoshimatsu. The master, Gihei, comes out.

GIHEI: There goes that cursed idiot with his screaming again. —Oh, it's Gōemon and Rikiya. Please come in.

GŌEMON *and* RIKIYA: Forgive the intrusion.

NARRATOR: When they have seated themselves Gōemon speaks.

GŌEMON: Our plans have gradually taken shape, thanks to your help. Yuranosuke should have come to thank you himself, but he's to leave for Kamakura almost immediately and he's so busy with one thing and another that he's sent his son Rikiya in his place to apologize for his discourtesy.

GIHEI: How considerate of him to think of that. I can well imagine how busy he must be, in view of his imminent departure.

RIKIYA: Yes, just as Gōemon said, Father has his hands full with the preparations for our departure early tomorrow morning. He took the liberty of sending me to express his gratitude. He also asked me to inquire if the baggage he requested you to send in the later shipments will have been loaded by this evening.

[69] The expression *hara ga heru* means "to be hungry." Igo mishears the name Hara Gōemon as Hara Heriemon and makes the bad joke.

GIHEI: Yes, the equipment you ordered has already been sent by sea in several shipments. The gauntlets, shin protectors, and other small items were packed into seven long boxes and were delivered to a captain whose ship, fortunately, is to sail this evening. I intend to send the remaining items—the masked lanterns and chain headbands—by land shortly.

RIKIYA: Have you heard that, Gōemon? We're tremendously obliged to you, sir.

GŌEMON: Indeed we are. Many townsmen benefited by Lord Enya's kindness, but Yura knew that Gihei of the Amagawaya has a chivalrous spirit not even a samurai could match. It was only natural he should have chosen you for this great service. But chain-mail vests and jointed ladders, not to mention lances and spears, are most unusual items of equipment. Didn't it arouse suspicion when you brought them?

GIHEI: No, I paid a deposit when I placed my order, but I didn't give the makers my address. I took away the equipment when it was ready, on payment of the balance. They have no idea who bought it or where I live.

RIKIYA: I see. An excellent plan! But, while we're on the subject, there's something I'd like to ask. How did you keep your employees from noticing when the equipment was brought into your place and packed for shipping?

GIHEI: That's a fair question. When I learned I was to be entrusted with this service, I sent my wife back to her parents, and I dismissed my employees one after the other, finding fault with all of them. The only ones left in the place now are a simpleton and my four-year-old son. There is no chance of word leaking out.

RIKIYA: You amaze me. I'll tell my father what you've told

me and set his mind at rest. Gōemon, don't you think we should be leaving?

GŌEMON: Yes, I think so. We're all impatient to start on our journey. Gihei, we'll be leaving you.

GIHEI: Good-by, sir. Please send my best regards to Yuranosuke.

GŌEMON: We will. Good-by.

NARRATOR: Exchanging farewells, they part. The two men leave for their lodgings, and Gihei is about to shut his gate when his father-in-law, Ōta Ryōchiku, appears.

RYŌCHIKU: Don't slam the gate on me. Are you at home?

NARRATOR: He marches right in and casts surreptitious glances around the place.

GIHEI: This is a surprise, Father. I'm glad to see you. I sent my wife to you the other day, thinking it would do her good. I'm sure you've been looking after her. Has she been taking her medicine?

RYŌCHIKU: Yes, she's been taking her medicine and eating normally.

GIHEI: That's splendid.

RYŌCHIKU: It's not splendid. In the old days, when I was back home, I used to receive a stipend from Ono Kudayū and I had a decent income. But now, when I can't even afford to keep a servant, you send me my daughter, though she's not suffering from any sickness worth mentioning, and you tell me to look after her. There must be something at the bottom of this. Be that as it may, if my daughter, in her inexperience, has been guilty of some misconduct, it's a disgrace to you and it leaves me no choice but to slit my wrinkled old belly. But I have a proposal to make. If—it's just for appearance's sake—you will pretend you've got rid of her and give her a letter of

divorce, you can always ask for her back whenever it suits
your convenience. One line will do—just dash it off.

NARRATOR: Gihei realizes that his father-in-law's offhand
manner of speech is deliberate, and that he has some
hidden motive. But if he refuses the request, his father-in-
law will send back his wife immediately; and if she returns, he will be breaking his word to those who trusted
him. He hesitates, drawn in both directions.

RYŌCHIKU: Are you willing, or aren't you? If you refuse, I
can't keep her a minute more. I'll send her back, and when
I do I'll worm my way in here with her. I'll settle here
and we'll both be a burden to you. Which is it—yes or
no? Give me your answer.

NARRATOR: Gihei is forced into a corner. He is chagrined to
think he has fallen victim to Ryōchiku's machinations,
but he cannot allow the great undertaking to be discovered. He pulls over his writing-box and quickly scrawls
a note.

GIHEI: Once I've given you this, Ryōchiku, you're no longer
my father and I'm no longer your son. I'll thank you
never to set foot in this house again. I know you have
some ulterior motive in asking for this letter of divorce,
and it exasperates me to have to give in to you. But take
it and go.

NARRATOR: He throws the note at Ryōchiku, who snatches it
up and thrusts it into his bosom.

RYŌCHIKU: Yes, you guessed right. I was told that *rōnin* have
been holding secret meetings here of late. I asked Sono,
but she said she knew nothing about it. It worried me to
leave my daughter in the hands of a son-in-law who might
be up to anything, for all I knew. Fortunately, I have been
approached by a certain distinguished person with an offer

of marriage. We agreed that Sono would marry him as soon as I got the letter of divorce. I've really put one over on you, and I'm satisfied!

GIHEI: Even supposing I hadn't already written the letter of divorce, I'd certainly have no affection left for a wife willing to desert the husband who had given her a child so she could marry another man. She can do as she pleases.

RYŌCHIKU: It's a father's prerogative to act as he thinks best. I'll see to it that she's married before this day is out.

GIHEI: I've had enough of your droning. Leave at once.

NARRATOR: He grasps the old man by the shoulder, kicks him out the door, and slams it on him. Ryōchiku rises uncertainly to his feet.

RYŌCHIKU: Gihei, you can manhandle me and fling me out the door all you want, but I've got the wedding money from the groom to keep me warm. And it's funny—being kicked seems to have cured me of my rheumatism!

NARRATOR: Glib as always, he keeps up a flow of spiteful mumbling as he makes his escape, rubbing his legs and back all the while.

The hour of the boar [70] has passed, and in the darkness of the clouded moon the houses all around are shrouded in sleep. A party of police makes for the house with truncheons, ropes, and long, hanging lanterns. They proceed cautiously, shielding the light. They beckon to an accomplice, apparently a spy, and whisper into his ear. He nods and pounds impatiently at the gate.

GIHEI: Who's there?

NARRATOR: He leans forward, ready to pounce on anyone who enters.

[70] From 10 P.M. to midnight.

SPY: I was here earlier this evening. I'm the skipper of the ship. There was a mistake in the freight charges. Open up, please.

GIHEI: What's all the commotion? I'm sure it's only a petty difference. Come back tomorrow.

SPY: No. The ship's sailing tonight. I can't put out to sea unless I get the account squared away.

NARRATOR: His voice is loud and Gihei, fearful lest the neighbors hear, goes to the gate and unsuspectingly opens it. He is instantly surrounded.

POLICE: We've got you. Don't make a move. We're here in the name of the government.

GIHEI: Why are you arresting me?

NARRATOR: He looks around him. The two policemen speak.

POLICE: You have the effrontery to ask why! We've been ordered to make an immediate arrest and to torture you until you confess you've purchased weapons and horse gear, and sent them by sea to Kamakura at the request of Ōboshi Yuranosuke, Enya Hangan's retainer. You can't escape. Tie his arms behind him!

GIHEI: The charge is absurd. I've not the faintest recollection of anything of the kind. You must have the wrong man.

NARRATOR: The policemen do not let him finish.

POLICE: Hold your tongue! We've incontrovertible evidence. Men, bring it here.

NARRATOR: The men, with a shout of obedience, bring in the long box wrapped in straw matting that was loaded aboard ship earlier that evening. At the sight Gihei's mind goes blank.

POLICE: Don't let him make a move!

NARRATOR: They brandish their truncheons as menials cut the ropes and start to open the long box. At that instant

Gihei flies at the box and, kicking the men aside, plants himself squarely on the lid.

GIHEI: What colossal impudence! This long box contains personal articles ordered by the wife of a certain daimyo, including pornographic books [71] for an armor chest. Her name is written on each article, even on the order for the erotic materials. If you open the box you will be exposing to public view the name of a great family. And seeing this name may endanger your own lives.

FIRST POLICEMAN: This guy gets more and more suspicious. It looks as if he won't confess quietly. Let's do what we agreed.

SECOND POLICEMAN: I'm with you.

NARRATOR: He runs into the next room and drags out Gihei's only son, Yoshimatsu.

POLICEMAN: Now, Gihei. Regardless of the contents of this box, the fact is you've joined forces with the league of Enya's *rōnin*. We're sure you know all about the secret plot to kill Moronao. You'd best tell us everything you know. If you won't talk, it's all over with your son. This is what we'll do—look!

NARRATOR: They press a naked sword to the young throat. Gihei is stunned, but his expression remains unaltered.

GIHEI: Ha-ha. I see you expect to extort a confession from me, the way you might from a woman or a child, by taking a hostage. But Gihei of the Amakawaya is a man. Not even love for my son can make me confess what I don't know. I know absolutely nothing about this, nothing whatsoever, and I'll go to hell before I confess what I don't

[71] It was the custom to put pornographic pictures in boxes of armor, etc., as a kind of magic for warding off fire.

know. If you don't like what I say, go ahead and kill my son before my eyes, yes, go ahead.

POLICEMAN: Why, you stubborn liar! You provided them with forty-six distinctively marked sets of ringed lances, guns, and chain-mail vests. Do you think we'll let you get away with pretending you know nothing? Confess, or we'll cut you up by inches, then slice you even thinner.

GIHEI: What a delightful suggestion! Go ahead and slice me. It's a merchant's business to sell everything, from crowns and court hats for the nobility down to straw sandals for scullery maids and apprentices. Of course I sell military equipment. If you think that's suspicious and should be investigated, there won't be anybody left in Japan by the time you get through. You can slice me inch by inch and truss me hand and foot, but I won't regret losing my life because I engaged in honest business. Go on, kill me! Stab my son before my eyes! Run him through! Tell me, when you slice a man by inches, do you start with the hands or do you split him through the chest first? Here, I offer you my shoulder bones and my spine—take your pick!

NARRATOR: He thrusts himself before them, then wrenches his son from their grip.

GIHEI: I'll show you my spirit won't be swayed by love of my son.

NARRATOR: He looks as if he intends to strangle the boy.

VOICE: Don't act so recklessly, Gihei! Wait a moment!

NARRATOR: Ōboshi Yuranosuke Yoshikane emerges from the long box, a sight to astonish Gihei. The policemen throw down their truncheons and ropes all at once and withdraw to a respectful distance, where they seat themselves.

Yuranosuke, sitting formally, bows to Gihei, touching his
hands to the floor.

YURANOSUKE: Such nobility of spirit has amazed me. Phrases
like "the lotus undefiled by the mud," or "gold among
the grains of sand" can aptly be applied to you. I judged
you were that kind of man, and that was why I asked so
great a service. I myself never had a particle of doubt
about you, but among our forty and more men some who
didn't know you wondered how Gihei of the Amakawaya,
a merchant by birth, would behave if he were captured
and interrogated. They thought you might talk. Others,
knowing you have an only son you dearly love, imagined
you, like any other father, would waver because of your
child. Doubts of every kind were expressed, and this uncertainty made our men restless. I had no choice. In order
to show my old companions the strength of your purpose
and set their minds at ease, I settled on the plan we used
tonight, though I realized how unfair it was. I most humbly beg your pardon for our heartless behavior. There's a
saying "among flowers the cherry blossom, and among
men the samurai," but no samurai could match your
determination. Even a man who could hold off a million
strong enemies might not be endowed with such a splendid character. If we borrow your spirit and make it our
model when we attack Moronao, how can we fail, even
if he's entrenched in the rocks or hidden in an iron cave?
They say there are no "men among men," but we have
found one for certain among the merchants. If we fail
to do you honor as the guardian deity of our league, the
god of our clan, our ingratitude will cost us the favor of
the gods. In times of stability, they say, no sages will appear. What a shame it is, what a great pity—if only our

late lord were alive he might reward your ability by making you the general of an army or entrusting you with the
government of a province, and never regret it. For those
of us before you—Ōwashi Bungo, Yazama Jūtarō, and
Kodera, Takamatsu, Horio, Itakura, and the rest—your
spirit is a miraculous medicine, a great physician who has
restored sight to damaged eyes. Thank you, thank you.

NARRATOR: They draw back respectfully and bow three times.

ALL: Forgive us for our outrageous behavior.

NARRATOR: They press their hands to the matting.

GIHEI: You embarrass me. Please lift your hands from the
floor. They say you must live with a man or ride on a
horse before you can tell their nature. I understand perfectly that these gentlemen, who know nothing about me,
should have been worried. I was formerly a poor man,
but I rose in the world thanks to the patronage I received from your province. When I heard what had happened to Lord Hangan, I shared your bitter rage. I racked
my brains to think of some way of wiping out this disgrace, but I was helpless as a sea turtle floundering on
the shore. Just when I had realized my own futility,
Yuranosuke asked my help. I accepted without a second
thought and took courage like yourselves. It's a miserable
thing to be a merchant. If I were a samurai, even if my
stipend had been a mere handful of rice, I would cling to
your sleeves and skirts when you set out on your mission
and go with you, if only to dip water for your tea when
you stop for a rest. But I cannot do even that. Yes, it's a
wretched thing to be a merchant. I see now how fortunate
a man is to know a master's kindness and the authority of
a sword. I envy you that you can lay down your lives for
them, and I hope that when you are serving your lord in

the afterworld you will find some occasion to inform him how Gihei showed his loyalty.

NARRATOR: These deeply felt words stir tears in his listeners, despite themselves; they can only grit their teeth. Yuranosuke answers at once.

YURANOSUKE: We are leaving tonight for Kamakura. Before a hundred days have passed our mission will be accomplished. I understand you've even divorced your wife. I deeply appreciate your sacrifice and I will do my best so that you can call her back soon. Please endure the hardship a little longer. Now I must bid you good-by.

NARRATOR: He rises to his feet.

GIHEI: You are about to start on a truly auspicious journey. Please let me offer you each a cup of saké.

YURANOSUKE: There's no need—

GIHEI: And, by way of celebrating the occasion, have some hand-cut noodles.[72]

YURANOSUKE: Hand-cut? A good omen! In that case, Ōwashi and Yazama, remain behind. But the men in the advance party must go fetch Gōemon and Rikiya and proceed to Sata Woods.

GIHEI: Come this way, please.

NARRATOR: The host leads the way. Yuranosuke, thinking that to refuse would be discourteous, goes inside with the other two men.

Osono, caught between father and husband, arrives as they depart, alone, a lantern in her hand, in the darkness of uncertainty that comes from love of her child. She knocks at the gate, hidden in the shadows.

---

[72] Te-uchi soba (hand-cut noodles) are so called in contrast with those ground out of a machine. "Hand-cut" suggests killing someone with one's hands and was therefore a favorable augury.

OSONO: Igo! Igo!

NARRATOR: Her voice wakens the dozing half-wit, and he rushes out.

IGO: Who called me? Was it a ghost? Or a wandering spirit?

OSONO: It's Sono. Open the gate.

IGO: That's what you say, but I feel something spooky in the air. Don't say "Boo!" and try to frighten me.

NARRATOR: He opens the door of the gate.

IGO: Oh, is it really you, ma'am? I'm glad to see you back. But if you go walking around all by yourself a mad dog's sure to bite you.

OSONO: Even if I were bitten to death by a dog, I'm sure I wouldn't suffer as much as I am doing now. My husband has divorced me! What a dreadful turn of events! Is the master asleep?

IGO: No.

OSONO: Is he away?

IGO: No.

OSONO: Then, what is he doing?

IGO: I don't know myself what he's up to, but early this evening the cat must've caught a mouse. Anyway, a lot of people came here and they were shouting, "We've caught him! We've caught him!" But I just pulled the covers over my head and went to sleep. Now the master's in the back room with those fellows and they're having a wild drinking party.

OSONO: I can't understand what's going on. And the boy, is he asleep?

IGO: Oh, yes, he's fast asleep.

OSONO: Has he been going to sleep with the master?

IGO: No.

OSONO: Has he been sleeping with you?

IGO: No, he sleeps all by himself.

OSONO: Why don't you stay with him and put him to sleep?

IGO: I wanted to, but all he did was cry and say he couldn't get any milk from either the master or myself.

OSONO: The poor child! I'm sure that's so. It's the one truthful thing you've said.

NARRATOR: She bursts into tears. As she stands by the gate, a rain never seen in the sky soaks her sleeves.

GIHEI: Igo, you good-for-nothing, where are you?

NARRATOR: The master Gihei comes out to summon him.

IGO: Here I am.

NARRATOR: He runs up and Gihei, giving him a black look out of the corner of his eye, exclaims.

GIHEI: Go inside, you dunce, and wait on the guests.

NARRATOR: Gihei sends Igo away with a scolding. He is about to bar the gate when Osono stops him.

OSONO: Master—there's something I must tell you. Please leave the gate open.

GIHEI: I have nothing to hear and nothing to say. You and your accomplices disgust me. Get out of here. You contaminate the place.

OSONO: I'll prove to you I'm not on my father's side. Look at this and you won't suspect me any more.

NARRATOR: She pushes a letter through a crack in the gate. As Gihei picks it up, his wife seizes the chance to slip in. Her husband glances over the letter.

GIHEI: Why, this is the letter of divorce I just gave you. What does this mean, returning it?

OSONO: What does it mean? How can you ask? You've always known about my father's nasty machinations. Why did you give him this letter, regardless of what he said? When he brought it home he announced he was marrying

me to another man, and, to my surprise, he began making
preparations for the event. I put him off his guard by pretending to be pleased, and then I stole the divorce papers
from his wallet and ran off with them.—Have you no
love left for Yoshimatsu? Did you intend to put him under
a stepmother once you'd divorced me? How cruel of you!

NARRATOR: She clings to him, weeping.

GIHEI: I'm the one who should be complaining. What did
you think my instructions meant when I sent you away?
I made it clear I was not divorcing you, but that certain
difficulties had come up and I wanted you to return for a
while to your father's house. I reminded you that Ryōchiku used to receive a stipend from Kudayū, and that I
could not confide in him as long as he and I were still
unreconciled. I asked you to pretend to be sick and not
to move around too freely, and urged you not to comb
your hair. Why did you forget my instructions? No man
would propose marriage to a woman whose hair was always in a mess. And how can you say you love Yoshimatsu? That idiot Igo spends the whole day long humor-
ing and cajoling the boy, but when night comes Yoshimatsu keeps asking for his mother. I trick him into going
to bed by telling him Mother will soon be home, but he
never sleeps soundly. If I scold him or try to browbeat him
into going to bed by spanking him or looking angry, he
doesn't cry but just sobs quietly. When I see him looking
that way, I feel as if my body is being broken apart at the
joints. It's more than I can bear. I know then why people
say a man knows his debt to his parents only when he's
had a child of his own, and I spend the night weeping
with remorse that this is my punishment for having been
a bad son to my own parents. Last night I took Yoshi-

matsu in my arms three times and went as far as the gate, thinking each time I would carry him to you. But he wouldn't be satisfied with just one night. We may have to say apart for fifty days or even a hundred days—there's no way of telling—and if he got used to being with you again it would make things all the harder later on. So I walked three *chō*, five *chō*, rocking him in my arms, patting him. I put him to sleep and laid him down quietly, holding him close to me. But in his dreams he groped for milk, and tired to suck. When I see how he misses you, even when you're separated for just a little while, I couldn't dream of keeping you apart for life. But I had no choice. That was why I wrote the note divorcing you and gave it to Ryōchiku. It would be improper for me to take it back on the sly, and your father would never forgive me. I'm not willing to do it. Take the letter and go. Consider that our relations were ordained in a former life, and that now I am dead, and everything is over.

NARRATOR: His resolute, masculine tone makes her all the sadder because she remembers his usual gentleness.

OSONO: If I remain in this house, I'll disgrace you. If I return to my parents, I must marry another man. What unhappiness for me to bear alone! This may be our final parting. Please wake up Yoshimatsu and let me see him a moment.

GIHEI: No. I'd feel all the sorrier for you afterwards if, no sooner than you had seen him, you had to leave. Besides, I have guests this evening. Please go quickly, without making such a fuss.

OSONO: I understand. But surely just one look at Yoshi-matsu—

GIHEI: Why can't you be a little stronger? Don't you see how much worse it would be afterwards?

NARRATOR: He lifts her up forcibly and, thrusting the divorce papers into her hand, propels her to the gate, then coldly pushes her outside.

GIHEI: If you love your son, you'll make your peace with Ryōchiku and persuade him to keep you until the spring. I'll think of something by then. But if you can't do that, this is the end.

NARRATOR: He shuts the door and goes inside.

OSONO: If I could do that, I shouldn't feel so miserable now. What a heartless man to have for a husband! You've not only divorced a blameless wife, but you won't even let me see my child. You're too unkind, too cruel. I won't budge until I see my child's face, no matter how long it takes.

NARRATOR: She pounds on the gate.

OSONO: In the name of human feelings, in the name of charity, open the gate! Please let me see him, even if he's asleep. I bow before you, I clasp my hands in supplication! You are inhuman!

NARRATOR: She throws herself to the ground and weeps, oblivious to what goes on around her.

OSONO: No, I won't be angry. I won't complain. If I looked Yoshimatsu in the face and he recognized me or clung to me, he'd never let me go, and I couldn't leave him either. But if I go back tonight, I must tonight become another man's wife. Fate will not let me live till tomorrow. It's good-by then, good-by forever.

NARRATOR: She presses her ear to the door, hoping she may perhaps hear her son's voice, or that she may still be permitted to see his face. But listen as she may, not a sound can be heard.

OSONO: There's no helping it. This is the end.

NARRATOR: She runs off in despair when a tall man, muffled to the eyes, blocks her way and seizes her. Before she can even cry out, the man draws his sword and brutally slashes off her hair at the roots. His next gesture is to snatch her purse and make off with it. She is helpless to resist this wanton display of force.

OSONO: How horrible! What an unspeakable thing to do! Who could be so cruel as to cut off my hair and steal my purse into the bargain? If the man was a thief after my combs and hair ornaments, I wish he had killed me instead.

NARRATOR: Startled by her cry of woe, Gihei begins to run to her before he realizes it, only to check himself, recalling that this is the time when a man's spirit may begin to waver; he can only grit his teeth. As he hesitates, a voice calls from inside.

VOICE: Where is the host? Gihei!

NARRATOR: Yuranosuke steps forward.

YURANOSUKE: I'll send you my thanks for your kind entertainment when I reach Kamakura. Please forward the rest of the baggage by fast messenger. I must leave before dawn breaks.

GIHEI: Yes, it's so late I can't press you to stay any longer. I hope you have a safe journey. I'll be waiting for the good news.

YURANOSUKE: I'll inform you by letter as soon as I arrive. Thank you again for all you've done. Words fail me. Yazama, Ōwashi—give our host the parting gifts.

NARRATOR: Bungo and Jūtarō come forward, each balancing a parcel on his fan, a makeshift presentation stand.

YURANOSUKE: This is for you, and this is for your wife, Osono. I'm sorry we can't offer anything better.

NARRATOR: He places them before Gihei, who changes color.

GIHEI: Are these the thanks you can't express in words? I didn't risk my life serving you because I hoped for a present. Do

you despise me as a merchant and suppose you can win me
over by the number of gold pieces you bestow?

YURANOSUKE: No. This is our farewell for this life. Your fate
is to remain in this world. That is why we are leaving this
small token of our feelings, in hopes you will look after
her ladyship Kaoyo.

NARRATOR: He starts out the gate. Gihei is all the more
incensed.

GIHEI: You've misjudged my nature and my character. The
way you've trampled on my honor is abominable, dis-
gusting.

NARRATOR: He kicks the gifts from him. The wrapping becomes undone and the contents spill out. His wife rushes
in.

OSONO: Look—here are my combs and hair ornaments, and
the hair shorn from my head. And look—this packet contains the divorce papers.

GIHEI: Then the man who cut off your hair—

YURANOSUKE: I sent Ōwashi Bungo around from the back
entrance to intercept your wife and cut off her hair at the
roots. I doubt that any father would attempt to offer in
marriage a daughter whose head was shaven like a nun's,
and it's even less likely any man would want such a bride.
It will take about a hundred days for her hair to grow
back, and less time than that for us to accomplish our mission. Once we've finished our business of killing the enemy
you can celebrate your reunion. Your wife will then have the
finest coiffure in the whole country if she uses the combs
and hair ornaments and this shorn hair as a switch. Until
then your son will have a nun for his wet nurse, a nun
engaged for a short term of service. Ōwashi Bungo and
Yazama Jūtarō will be her guarantors. These two men
will bear witness to our league that she will not reveal our

secret. And, even though I shall be in the world of the
dead, I promise to serve as go-between for your new
marriage, Gihei.

GIHEI: What great generosity! Thank him, wife.

OSONO: You are the savior of my life.

YURANOSUKE: There is no need to thank me. I've given you
one hair in return for your gift of nine oxen.[73] Gihei has
said that he would have gone with us on our journey if he
weren't a merchant. Fortunately, it will still be possible.
We've decided to make our attack by night. When we
break into the enemy's stronghold we will use the name of
your shop, Amakawaya, as our passwords. If one man
challenges the other with *ama*, he will be answered with
kawa, and if the forty and more men of our league all use
these words *ama* and *kawa*,[74] it will be the same as if you
were present at our night attack. The character *gi* in your
name Gihei is the same as in *gishin* [righteous retainers],
and the *hei* means that we shall smoothly and easily carry
out our mission. But now we must leave you.

NARRATOR: These passwords will be used in ages to come,
with *yama* instead of *ama*, and Yuranosuke's strategy,
worthy of Sun and Wu, will be known popularly as
Chūshingura, or The Treasury of Loyal Retainers. In this
uncertain world even words depart from their original
meanings, as now the warriors depart on their journey,
bidding the others sad farewell.

[73] A Chinese expression meaning to repay an enormous gift with an
extremely small return present.

[74] *Ama* means "heaven," and *kawa* means "river." The passwords *yama*
(mountain) and *kawa* were used as recently as World War II, but it
is doubtful that, as the author claims in the next speech, they were
derived from *ama* and *kawa*.

Act Eleven

NARRATOR: The pliant can control the unyielding, and the weak the strong: this was the secret doctrine transmitted by Shih-kung to Chang Liang.[75] Ōboshi Yuranosuke, the retainer of Enya Hangan Takasada, obeying this teaching, has ordered that the decks of the fishing boats boarded by his forty and more brave men be covered with thick rush mats, and that the boats be rowed towards the rocky shore of Cape Inamura,[76] which is unlikely to be guarded. The first to set foot on shore is Ōboshi Yuranosuke Yoshikane, the second, Hara Gōemon, and the third, Ōboshi Rikiya. Following them come Takemori Kitahachi and Katayama Genta. The men in the leading boats and those following move steadily ashore, not breaking their ranks. Next ashore are Okuyama Magoshichi and Tsugita Gorō. The seven men stand in a row, the letters on their cloaks spelling out i-ro-ha-ni-ho-he-to.[77] Katsuta, Hayami, Tōnomori, the

75 Chang Liang was said to have learned military strategy from the textbook San Lüeh given him by an old man. (See Watson, tr., Records, I, 135.)

76 A place on the coast southwest of Kamakura.

77 These are the first seven syllables of the iroha song which uses all forty-seven kana once.

171

famed Katayama Gengo and Ōwashi Bungo who carries
a huge mallet, Yoshida and Okazaki form *chi-ri-nu-ru-wo-
wa-ka*. The young men are led by Kodera, Tatekawa Jim-
bei, Fuwa, Maebara, Fukagawa Yajirō, Kawase Chūdayū,
who lands with a half-sized bow,[78] his specialty, under his
arm, and Ōboshi Sebei, who shines like a star in the sky:
they form the third group, *yo-ta-re-so-tsu-ne-na*. Then follow *ra-mu-u-i-no-o-ku*: Okumura, Okano, the elder Kodera
son, Nakamura, Yajima, Maki, and Hiraga. Then, lined
up in the morning mist, *ya-ma-ke-fu-ko-e-te* are Ashino
and Sugano, Chiba and Muramatsu, Murahashi Denji,
Shiota, and Akane, armed with spears. The next group
includes Isogawa, who carries a forked lance, Tōmatsu,
Sugino, Mimura no Jirō, Kimura, who has a jointed ladder
ready, Senzaki Yagorō, the Horii brothers Yasō and
Yakurō, who carry great bamboo poles eight feet long
strung with bowstrings, the plan Yuranosuke hit on in the
gay quarters when pretending to be drunk. The rear guard
consists of Yazama Jūtarō and, far behind, humbling
himself, Teraoka Heiemon. Altogether they make forty-six
men, each with a badge on his sleeve marked with his
common and formal names. They wear black cloaks and
breeches of mail, and breastplates over their loyal hearts.
Truly these men form a copybook of loyalty.[79]

YURANOSUKE: Don't forget the passwords *ama* and *kawa*,

[78] A bow used for shooting from a sitting position.

[79] There is a play here on "copybook of loyalty" and "copybook of
the *kana*," in other words, a penmanship book. *Kanadehon* (copybook
of *kana*) figures at the head of the title of the play. It will be noted,
however, that the names of only forty-five men are listed here, and not
forty-six, as stated. Even adding the name of the dead Hayano Kampei,
there is still one short of the forty-seven required. The names also
conflict in two instances with those mentioned in Act X.

the name of Gihei's shop. Follow the plans we agreed on. One party, headed by Yazama, Senzaki, Kodera, and my son Rikiya, will break in by the front gate. Gōemon and I will push our way in through the back gate. When I blow the signal whistle it will mean the time has come to scale the walls. Remember, we need take only one head.

NARRATOR: In response to these commands from Yuranosuke, as one man they direct looks of fierce hatred at the distant mansion, then separate into parties bound for the front and back gates.

Kō no Moronao, the governor of Musashi, unaware of these developments, has been drinking, his vigilance relaxed, reassured by the stories he has heard of Yuranosuke's dissipation. Geishas and prostitutes dance and sing at his bidding as he carouses, ignorant of his fate, with Yakushiji as his chief guest. In the end they all fall asleep; men and women sprawl indiscriminately together, oblivious to everything. The only sound is the watchman's clappers as he makes his rounds. The attacking parties at front and back gates make final arrangements at the same time, and two fearless men, Yazama and Senzaki, creep up to the front gate to observe conditions inside. They hear a distant sound of clappers, no doubt the night watchman's, and, judging this to be the opportune moment, they lean against the high wall the jointed ladders they have kept in readiness. Nimble as spiders, they race up the wall, as though headed for the clouds, and soon reach the roof. The sound of the clappers is now near at hand as they lightly leap down on the other side. The watchman, catching sight of them, runs up with a shout of "Who's there?" They grab the man and force him down to the ground, then bind him at wrists and elbows. "He'll make a

good guide," they think, so they gag him and, tying the
ends of the ropes to their waists, take his clappers and
boldly make the rounds of the guardrooms, observing the
lay of the land. Soon the whistle is heard from the back
gate, and the two men, deciding the moment has come,
time their shouts of the passwords *ama* and *kawa* to the
beat of the clappers as they unfasten the door bolt and
fling open the main gate. The party headed by Rikiya,
including Sugino, Kimura, and Mimura, rushes in, but
they can tell at a glance that the mansion is securely pro-
tected on all sides by shutters. "Now is the time to put
into practice what my father taught me about the snow-
laden bamboo," Rikiya thinks, and he commands the
others. They insert bamboo poles bent by bowstrings under the lintels and thresholds of the shutters, then all
together, at a cry of "one, two, three," cut the bowstrings.
The lintels rise and the thresholds fall, and the shutters,
forced from their grooves, clatter down one after the
other. "Now let's break in!" they cry, and exchanging
shouts of *ama* and *kawa*, they burst inside. "It's a night
attack!" the alarm goes up, and men race out with torches
and lanterns. From the back gate too the attackers pour
in. Gōemon on one side and Yuranosuke on the other,
seated on camp stools, direct the fighting. Though few in
number, these are courageous men, deadly determined to
succeed this night and employing every secret tactic.

YURANOSUKE: Kill Moronao! Pay no attention to anyone
else.

NARRATOR: He and Gōemon give orders to men on all sides,
and the hot-blooded youths tangle and clash again and
again.

The neighbor to the north is Nikki, the governor of

Harima, and the neighbor to the south, Ishidō Umanojō. Both neighbors send soldiers to the housetops to find out what is happening, and their lanterns shine like stars.

SAMURAI: What are all those wild noises coming from your mansion? We hear shouts, swords clashing, the cries of archers. What's going on? Is it a drunken brawl? Have bandits broken in? Or has some sudden decree come from the government? Our master commands us to find out.

NARRATOR: Their voices ring out loudly. Yuranosuke answers at once.

YURANOSUKE: We are the retainers of Enya Hangan. Forty and more of us are fighting with every means at our disposal to avenge our master. I am Ōboshi Yuranosuke, and this is Hara Gōemon. We have no quarrel with Takauji or his brother. Nor do we bear any grudge against either Lord Nikki or Lord Ishidō, so we promise to do nothing irresponsible. I have ordered our men to take the strictest precautions against fire, so you need have no worries on that account. We ask only that you peaceably refrain from interfering. But if you feel you can't turn a deaf ear to what happens in a neighbor's house and send in reinforcements, we will have no choice but to retaliate with our arrows.

NARRATOR: The men of both houses, hearing this bold proclamation, shout back.

SAMURAI: What superb courage! Every man who serves a master should behave as you are doing. Call if you have any need of us. Withdraw the lanterns!

NARRATOR: All at once the neighborhood becomes still. During the fighting, which has lasted about two hours, barely two or three of the attackers have been slightly wounded, but the enemy casualties are beyond numbering. Nevertheless, the enemy general Moronao eludes detection. The foot soldier Teraoka Heiemon runs around the mansion, searching the rooms and probing with his lance the ceilings, the floorboards, and even the wells, but no one can tell where Moronao has gone. Now Heiemon looks into what seems to be Moronao's bedchamber. The bedclothes are still warm, despite the cold of the night, and he realizes it cannot have been long since Moronao fled. He rushes outside, afraid Moronao has somehow escaped the house, when a voice calls.

JŪTARŌ: Heiemon, wait!

NARRATOR: Yazama Jūtarō Shigeyuki drags in Moronao, all but carrying him in his arms.

JŪTARŌ: Hear me, everyone. I found him hiding in the woodshed and took him alive.

NARRATOR: The others all rush up, bolstered in spirits like a flower touched with dew.

YURANOSUKE: Nobly done, a tremendous feat. But we mustn't kill him hastily. After all, he served for a time as a high officer of the government. The proper decorum must be observed even when killing him.

NARRATOR: Taking him from Jūtarō, he makes Moronao sit in the place of honor.

YURANOSUKE: We, who are merely retainers of a retainer, have broken into your mansion and performed acts of violence because we wished to avenge our master's death. I beg you to forgive this gross discourtesy, and to give us your head without offering resistance.

NARRATOR: Moronao, master of deceit that he is, betrays no fear.

MORONAO: I understand. I have long been expecting this. Take my head.

NARRATOR: He puts Yuranosuke off guard with these words, only suddenly to draw his sword and strike at him. Yuranosuke wards off the blow and twists Moronao's arm.

YURANOSUKE: Ha—what a touching display of resistance! All of you, now is the moment to satisfy our long-accumulated hatred!

NARRATOR: Yuranosuke strikes the first blow, and the forty and more men raise shouts of joy and celebrate, as a blind sea tortoise might rejoice to find a floating log, or as they themselves might rejoice on seeing the flower of the *udonge*, that blooms only once in three thousand years.[80] They jump and leap in exuberance, and using the dagger their lord left behind as a remembrance of him, they cut off Moronao's head. In their high spirits they even dance. It was to see this head, and for no other reason, that they deserted their wives, separated from their children, lost their old parents. What a glorious day this is! They beat the head, they bite at it, and weep for joy, a moving sight because so completely understandable. Yuranosuke takes from his breast the memorial tablet of his late master and places it on a table in the alcove. He cleanses Moronao's head of the bloodstains and offers it before the tablet, then burns the incense he has carried inside his helmet. He steps back respectfully and bows three times, then nine times, before the tablet.

YURANOSUKE: I humbly report to the sacred spirit of my late master, Renshōin Kenri Daikoji.[81] I have, using the dagger you bestowed on me after you committed *seppuku*, and obeying your command to appease your spirit, cut off Moronao's head and offered it before your memorial tab-

---

[80] Another reference to the *udonge* flower. See above, n. 32.

[81] Enya Hangan's posthumous Buddhist name.

let. Please accept it from your resting place under the sod.

NARRATOR: In tears he offers his prayers.

YURANOSUKE: Come, each of you, burn incense before him.

OTHERS: You burn incense first. You have been our commanding general.

YURANOSUKE: Yazama Jūtarō, you offer incense ahead of me.

JŪTARŌ: No, that's unthinkable. It's embarrassing to be singled out ahead of the others.

YURANOSUKE: I'm not showing any partiality. The forty and more of us are all laying down our lives for the satisfaction of taking Moronao's head. But you were the one among us to find him in his place of hiding and capture him alive. It shows, Yazama, how dear you are to the sacred spirit of our master Enya. We envy you. What do you say, gentlemen?

SAMURAI: We agree.

JŪTARŌ: But I don't know what—

YURANOSUKE: We're wasting time.

JŪTARŌ: In that case, by your leave.

NARRATOR: He lights the first stick of incense.

JŪTARŌ: The second must be offered by Yuranosuke. Stand, please.

YURANOSUKE: No, still another man must burn incense before me.

JŪTARŌ: Who is it? Which of us?

NARRATOR: Ōboshi takes from his breast a wallet of checkered cloth.[82]

YURANOSUKE: The second of the loyal retainers to burn incense will be this last remnant of Hayano Kampei. He was

[82] The dramatist seems to have forgotten that the cloth was previously (in the sixth act) described as striped. Presumably this lapse was occasioned by the multiple authorship.

not allowed to join our league because of an indiscretion, but hoping at least to be one of those to erect the monument, he sold his wife to raise money. His father-in-law was killed because of this money, and the money itself was rejected by us. In despair, he cut his belly and died. How bitterly humiliated Kampei must have felt at the time, how mortified! Rejecting his money was the greatest mistake of my life. Never for a moment have I forgotten that it was I who caused him to die that wretched death, and I've never let the wallet leave my person. Tonight the wallet accompanied us on our attack. Heiemon, he was your sister's husband. Let him burn incense.

NARRATOR: He throws the wallet at Heiemon, who lifts it to his brow with a respectful murmur.

HEIEMON: I am sure Kampei in his grave must be grateful. It is the greatest good fortune that could come to him.

NARRATOR: He places the wallet on the incense burner and proclaims.

HEIEMON: The second to offer incense is Hayano Kampei Shigeuji.

NARRATOR: His voice trembles with tears, and the others feel their hearts must break with regret. At this moment, to their astonishment, they hear noises of men and horses. The mountains and valleys resound with attacking drums and the din of the battle cries. Yuranosuke remains unperturbed.

YURANOSUKE: Moronao's men seem to have attacked. What use would it be to increase our sins?

NARRATOR: As they wait, prepared for death, Momonoi Wakasanosuke rushes in, afraid he has come too late.

WAKASANOSUKE: Ōboshi—Moronao's younger brother Moroyasu is attacking now at the front gate. If you commit suicide here, people will slander you even in generations to come, saying you were afraid of the enemy. You should withdraw to Lord Enya's family temple, the Kōmyōji.

NARRATOR: Yuranosuke nods.

YURANOSUKE: Yes, it would be best to end our lives before our master's tomb. We will withdraw, as you suggest. I ask that you protect us from the rear.

NARRATOR: Hardly has he spoken when Yakushiji Jirō and Sagisaka Bannai, who must have been hiding in the mansion, suddenly leap out.

YAKUSHIJI *and* BANNAI: Curse you, Ōboshi, we won't let you get away!

NARRATOR: They fall on him from left and right, but Rikiya parries their thrusts. For a while they fight together but, seeing his chance, Rikiya strikes with his broadsword and Yakushiji, slashed slantwise through the shoulder, breathes his last. With his next sweep of the sword Rikiya lops off Sagisaka Bannai's legs [83] and he helplessly expires on the spot. All raise a shout of acclaim, "Well done! Well done!" and this praise will be echoed through ages to come for these loyal retainers, a sign His Majesty's reign will last forever.

We have recorded here their glory, ever renewed like the leaves of the bamboo.[84]

Takeda Izumo

Miyoshi Shōraku

Namiki Senryū

[83] Another play on the name Sagisaka is imbedded in the text: the heron has no tail, so when Sagisaka (Heron-Slope) has his legs cut off he has nothing to rest on.

[84] A reference is made here to the Takemoto Theater. The name Takemoto means "base of the bamboo" and the theater's crest consists of bamboo leaves. In other words, the long prosperity of this theater, where the play is now being offered, is celebrated.

Works Consulted

Akō Gijin Sansho. 2 vols. + supplementary vol. Tokyo, Kokusho Kankōkai, 1911.

A collection of the basic documents concerning the historical events that inspired the play.

Gunji Masakatsu. *Kabuki.* Translated by John Bester. Tokyo and Palo Alto, Kodansha International Ltd., 1969.

Includes many photographs of the Kabuki version of the play.

Brandon, James R., ed. *Chūshingura: Studies in Kabuki and the Puppet Theater.* Honolulu, University of Hawaii Press, 1982.

Donald Keene's essay is "Variations on a Theme: Chūshingura," pp. 1–21.

Inouye, Jukichi. *Chushingura or Forty Seven Ronin.* Tokyo, Nakanishi-ya, 1910.

A good, if rather old-fashioned translation of the original play, together with an introduction describing its background.

Jippensha Ikku. *Chūshingura Okame Hyōban* (in *Akō Fukushū Zenshū*), Teikoku Bunko series. Tokyo, Hakubunkan, 1895.

A collection of informative materials, arranged in anecdotal form, concerning the writing of *Chūshingura*.

Kawatake Shigetoshi and Fujino Yoshio. *Kanadehon Chūshingura Hyōkai.* Nagoya, Kengaku Shobō, 1953.

Text of the original play with fairly useful explanatory materials.

Kawatake Toshio and Hayashi Kakichi. *Chūshingura.* Tokyo, Kōdansha, 1967.

Many colored photographs of Kabuki productions of the play.

Keene, Donald. *Bunraku, the Puppet Theatre of Japan.* Tokyo and Palo Alto, Kodansha International Ltd., 1965.

Includes photographs of the puppet theatre productions of the play.

Matsushima Eiichi. *Chūshingura*. Tokyo, Iwanami Shoten, 1964.
Treats both the historical events and the composition of the play.

Minamoto Ryōen. *Giri to Ninjō*. Tokyo, Chūō Kōron Sha, 1969.
An excellent study of the two concepts underlying much literature of the Tokugawa period.

Mitamura Engyo. *Akō Gishi*. Tokyo, Seiabō, 1958.
A delightful book of gossip about the historical events.

Mueller, Jacqueline. "A Chronicle of Great Peace Played Out on a Chessboard: Chikamatsu Monzaemon's *Goban Taiheiki*." *Harvard Journal of Asiatic Studies* 46 (1): 22–267.

Nakamura Nakazō. *Temae Miso* (ed. Gunji Masakatsu). Tokyo, Seiabō, 1969.
Memoirs of a great Kabuki actor. Full of interesting material.

Onoe Kikugorō. *Gei*. Tokyo, Kaizō Sha, 1947.
Includes many valuable insights into the Kabuki performance of *Chūshingura*.

Otoba Hiromu. *Jōruri Shū*, I, in Nihon Koten Bungaku Taikei series. Tokyo, Iwanami Shoten, 1960.
The standard text of the play, with woefully inadequate notes.

Ozawa Yoshikuni, ed. *Chūshingura Jōruri Shū*, in Teikoku Bunko series. Tokyo, Hakubunkan, 1929.
Contains 14 *jōruri* plays on the *Chūshingura* theme.

Shikitei Samba. *Chūshingura Henkichi Ron* (in *Kokkei Meisaku Shū*), in Teikoku Bunko series. Tokyo, Hakubunkan, 1894.
A satirical reevaluation of the characters in the play.

Shikitei Samba. *Ukiyo-buro* (ed. Nakamura Michio), in Nihon Koten Bungaku Taikei series. Tokyo, Iwanami Shoten, 1957.

Shioya, Sakae. *Chûshingura, an Exposition*. Tokyo, The Hokuseido Press, 1940.
A retelling of the historical events, followed by a summary of the play.

Sonoda Tamio. *Jōruri Sakusha no Kenkyū*. Tokyo, Tōkyōdō, 1944.
Contains an interesting but outdated analysis of *Chūshingura*.

Takano Masami. *Chikamatsu Monzaemon Shū*, in Nihon Koten Zensho series. 3 vols. Tokyo, Asahi Shimbun Sha, 1950–52.
A generous sampling of Chikamatsu's plays with some notes.

Tamura Eitarō. *Akō Rōshi*. Tokyo, Yūsankaku, 1969.

An attempt to "debunk" the usual historical accounts.

Toita Yasuji. *Chūshingura*. Tokyo, Sōgensha, 1957.

Especially useful for the descriptions of the different Kabuki traditions of performing the play.

Tsurumi Makoto. *Takeda Izumo Shū*, in Nihon Koten Zensho series. Tokyo, Asahi Shimbun Sha, 1956.

Yamamoto Jirō and Gunji Masakatsu, eds. *Kanadehon Chūshingura*, in Kabuki Meisaku Sen series. Tokyo, Sōgensha, 1957.

The Kabuki version of the play, plus a useful "explanation" by Toita Yasuji.

Yokoyama Tadashi. *Jōruri Ayatsuri Shibai no Kenkyū*. Tokyo, Kazama Shobō, 1963.

A most impressive study of *jōruri* plays.

Yuda Yoshio, "Takeda Izumo no Shūmei to Sakuhin," in *Kinsei Bungei*, I (no. 1, Oct., 1954).

A brilliant article that established the identity of Takeda Izumo II, after his existence had been questioned by some scholars.